UK Ninja Dual Zone Air Fryer Cookbook For Beginners

1900 Days Affordable and Crispy Recipesfor Beginners with Expert Tips to Master Double Zone Air Fryer

Rachel S. Byrnes

Contents

Getting to Know your Ninja Foodi Dual Zone

As a cooking enthusiast who has previously owned a restaurant in the UK, I am excited to introduce you to my favorite kitchen appliance - the Ninja Air Fryer.

In this book, you will find all the information you need about the Ninja Air Fryer. In my opinion, it is a miraculous little helper in the kitchen that can do wonders for your cooking.

The Ninja Air Fryer is one of my top three favorite air fryers due to its versatility and ability to cook various types of food at the same time. It is reasonably priced and doesn't take up too much space in the kitchen.

Obesity is a significant health concern in the UK, and the Ninja Air Fryer can help address this issue by reducing the fat content in meals by up to 75%. For instance, a recent study shows that air frying chicken wings using the Ninja Air Fryer reduces fat content by 60% compared to deep-frying, making it a healthier option for those looking to indulge in this popular snack.

The Ninja Dual Zone Air Fryer is an innovative kitchen appliance that features two ceramic-coated baskets, making it a perfect addition to any household that loves to cook. The baskets

are non-stick and dishwasher safe, ensuring easy and convenient cleaning after use. Additionally, the baskets are free from harmful chemicals such as PFOA and PTFE, which makes them safe for cooking various types of food. The digital control panel on the Ninja Dual Zone Air Fryer is designed to make cooking a breeze. With this feature, it is easy to set the temperature and cooking time, which can be adjusted to suit the type of food you are preparing.

In summary, the Ninja Dual Zone Air Fryer is a versatile and powerful appliance for home cooks. Its features make it a top pick for busy households, as it allows you to prepare multiple dishes at once with minimal mess and hassle. With its convenient, dishwasher-safe components, it's also easy to clean up after meals. Whether you're cooking for one or catering to multiple hungry mouths, this air fryer has got you covered!

6 Features That Will Make You Want a Ninja Foodi Dual Zone

The Ninja Air Fryer has gained a following among home chefs and boasts favorable reviews for its performance, versatility, and multi-functional features. In this review, we will take a closer look at the key elements of the Ninja Dual Zone Air Fryer.

At the heart of the air fryer is the main unit that houses the heating elements, controls, and other internal components. Additionally, the Ninja Dual Zone Air Fryer features two cooking baskets, which enable simultaneous cooking of two different dishes. The baskets are equipped with a non-stick coating and a handle that makes it easy to remove them from the main unit. The capacity of both the drawers and baskets is also substantial, making it an ideal choice for preparing meals for a complete family.

Moreover, the air fryer comes with two crisper plates that can replace the cooking baskets. These plates are specially designed to provide the same crispy texture you would get from deep-frying, while using less oil. Another noteworthy feature of the Ninja Dual Zone Air Fryer is the drip tray, which collects any excess oil or grease that drips from the food during cooking. And, it's removable and dishwasher-safe.

Air Frying: The air frying feature is the most popular function of the Ninja Air Fryer, as it allows for healthier cooking by using little to no oil. This feature is perfect for making crispy chicken wings, fries, or even vegetables. The powerful fan in the fryer circulates hot air around the food, cooking it to perfection without the need for excess oil.

Roasting: The roasting feature of the Ninja Air Fryer is perfect for cooking meats such as a whole chicken or turkey. With its easy-to-use controls, you can set the temperature and timer and let the machine do the rest. You can also use this feature to roast vegetables or potatoes with minimal effort.

Baking: The baking feature of the Ninja Air Fryer is ideal for all those dessert lovers out there, who can now use this appliance to cook cakes, bread, cookies and pies with even browning and cooking. Its compact size makes it perfect for small batches of baked goods.

Air Broiling: The air broiling feature of the Ninja Air Fryer is an added bonus that not many air fryers have. With this feature, you can cook meats and fish to a crispy exterior while keeping the natural juices intact for a flavorful and juicy meal.

Reheating: The reheating feature is another popular function of the Ninja Air Fryer. It allows you to reheat leftovers or frozen foods like pizza or chicken tenders, with ease and convenience. Your reheated food will taste fresh and delicious, without sacrificing taste or texture.

Dehydrating: The dehydrating feature is useful for anyone who enjoys making their dried fruits or jerky at home. With the Ninja Air Fryer's low-temperature settings and powerful fan, you can easily dehydrate your favorite fruits or meats without having to invest in a separate dehydrator.

The Key Benefits of the Ninja Dual Zone Air Fryer

When it comes to cooking, most of us prefer an appliance that is not only reliable but also versatile. This is where the Ninja air fryer comes in, as it offers a range of benefits to make your cooking experience easier and better.

Multifunctionality

The Ninja air fryer is more than just an air fryer; it is a multi-purpose cooking appliance that allows you to grill, roast, bake, and dehydrate food as well. With its versatile functions, you can cook different kinds of recipes effortlessly, making your life easier in the kitchen.

Safe and reliable

Safety should be a top priority when it comes to any kitchen appliance, and the Ninja air fryer doesn't disappoint in this area. It features an auto shut-off system that ensures your food doesn't overcook or burn.

Healthier lifestyle choice

People nowadays are more health-conscious and prefer cooking methods that require less oil and fat. The Ninja air fryer is an excellent alternative to traditional deep fryers as it uses hot air to cook the food instead of oil.

Easy to operate and clean

The Ninja air fryer's intuitive digital control panel makes it easy for anyone to operate the appliance. With just a push of a button, you can set the cooking time and temperature, making the cooking process hassle-free. Cleaning the appliance is also easy since it features a non-stick surface that makes cleaning up a breeze.

Suitable for everyone

Whether you're a vegan, meat-lover, or follow a specific diet, the Ninja air fryer is suitable for everyone.

Cost-effective

Investing in a Ninja air fryer is not only beneficial in terms of convenience and cooking, but it is also a cost-effective option. Additionally, since it uses less oil and electricity, you will see a reduction in your energy bills too.

Cons of using Ninja dual-zone air fryer

There are several cons to consider when using the Ninja dual-zone air fryer.

Firstly, it is quite large and takes up a lot of counter space, which may be a problem for people with smaller kitchens.

Secondly, it can be quite noisy when in use, which may be disruptive to some users.

Additionally, the air fryer may not cook food evenly, resulting in some parts being overcooked while others are undercooked. This can be especially problematic for foods that require precise cooking times and temperatures.

The air fryer also has a non-stick coating, which can wear off over time and potentially release harmful chemicals into your food.

Finally, the Ninja dual-zone air fryer is relatively expensive compared to other air fryers on the market, which may deter some consumers from purchasing it.

It is important to weigh the pros and cons before deciding if the Ninja dual-zone air fryer is the right appliance for your needs. While there are many benefits to using this air fryer, such as its versatility, ease of use, and ability to cook food quickly and evenly, it is also quite large and noisy, may not cook food evenly, has a non-stick coating that can wear off over time, and is relatively expensive compared to other air fryers on the market. Therefore, it is important to carefully consider these potential drawbacks in order to make an informed decision about whether or not to purchase the Ninja dual-zone air fryer.

Cleaning & Maintaining

How to clean the Ninja Dual Zone Air Fryer?

- Just like any other kitchen appliance, you must keep your Ninja air fryer clean in order for it to function properly and last a long time. Properly maintaining the equipment for its maximum benefits is crucial. Here are some steps to follow:
- First, start by unplugging the air fryer and allowing it to cool down completely. Never attempt to clean it while it's still hot as this can lead to burns or damage to the unit.
- Remove the frying basket and drip pan from the air fryer.
- Add warm water and a few drops of dish soap to the sink/dish rack and use a non-abrasive sponge or cloth to wash the basket and pan. Be sure to remove any food residue or grease that may have accumulated during cooking.
- If the frying basket has stubborn stains, soak it in warm soapy water for a few minutes to make

cleaning easier.

- Rinse the basket and drip pan under running water and dry thoroughly with a clean towel.
- To clean the exterior of the air fryer, wipe it down with a damp cloth or sponge. Avoid using abrasive cleaners or steel wool pads, which can scratch the surface.
- Once everything is clean and dry, reassemble the frying basket and drip pan back into the air fryer
- For maintaining the air fryer, regularly check and clean the air intake vents on the side and bottom of the unit. This ensures that air can flow freely through the appliance and prevents overheating.
- Always follow the manufacturer's instructions for use and maintenance to ensure safe and proper operation.

Maintaining your ninja dual zone air fryer

In order to keep your air fryer working efficiently and effectively, it's important to properly maintain it. Here are some tips and suggestions on how to maintain your Ninja Dual Zone Air Fryer.

- Regularly clean the air fryer after each use to prevent build-up of food debris and grease.
- Avoid using metal utensils or abrasive sponges when cooking in the air fryer, as they may scratch the non-stick coating.
- Always make sure the air fryer is fully assembled before use.
- Avoid overfilling the basket or cooking pot, as this may cause the food to cook unevenly and prevent proper air circulation.
- When storing the air fryer, make sure it is completely cool and dry.

- Store the air fryer in a clean, dry area away from moisture and direct sunlight.
- Avoid stacking heavy objects on top of the air fryer, as this may damage it.

Additional Tips And Tricks

If you're new to the world of air fryers, the Ninja Dual Zone Air Fryer is a great place to start. This versatile appliance can cook anything from crispy chicken wings to perfectly roasted vegetables. Here are some tips to help you get the most out of your Ninja Dual Zone Air Fryer:

·Use the pre-set cooking programs

The Ninja Dual Zone Air Fryer comes with pre-set cooking programs for various foods like chicken, fish, fries, and more. These programs are designed to cook your food to perfection and take the guesswork out of cooking.

·Rotate the Basket

It is important to rotate the air fryer basket halfway through the cooking process to ensure that your food is cooked evenly. This will prevent the food from sticking to the basket and ensure that it is fully cooked on all sides.

·Don't Overcrowd the Basket

One of the biggest mistakes people make when using an air fryer is overcrowding the basket. This can result in uneven cooking and a soggy texture.

·Use Oil Sparingly

While the Ninja Dual Zone Air Fryer can cook with little or no oil, a small amount can enhance the flavor and texture of your food. Just be sure to use it sparingly to avoid making your food oily and greasy.

·Experiment with Different Foods

The Ninja Dual Zone Air Fryer is versatile and can cook a wide range of foods. Don't be afraid to experiment with different food items and see what works best for you. You may be surprised by what you can cook in an air fryer!

·Choose the Right Cooking Temperature

You can refer to the recipe book that comes with

the air fryer for the recommended temperature settings for different foods.

·Use accessories

The Ninja Dual Zone Air Fryer comes with several accessories like a crisper plate, baking tray, and wire rack. Experiment with these accessories to cook different types of food.

·Start with Simple Recipes

As a beginner, it's always best to start with simple recipes that don't require much preparation. This will help you get a better understanding of how the air fryer works.

Frequently Asked Questions

1.What types of food can I cook with the Ninja Dual Zone Air Fryer?

The Ninja Dual Zone Air Fryer can cook a wide range of foods, such as chicken wings, french fries, vegetables, fish fillets, and even desserts like donuts and cakes.

2.Can I cook frozen foods in the Ninja Dual Zone Air Fryer?

Yes, you can. However, you may need to add a few extra minutes to the cooking time to ensure the food is thoroughly cooked.

3.Can I use aluminum foil in the Ninja Dual Zone Air Fryer?

Yes, you can use aluminum foil in the Ninja Dual Zone Air Fryer. However, make sure to use only a small amount and avoid covering the entire basket as it may prevent proper air circulation.

4.How much food can I cook in the Ninja Dual Zone Air Fryer?

The Ninja Dual Zone Air Fryer has a 6-quart capacity for the cooking basket and a 4-quart capacity for the crisper plate.

5.Is it possible to cook multiple foods at once in the air fryer?

Yes, you can cook multiple foods at once using the dual-zone feature of the Ninja Dual Zone Air Fryer. Just make sure that the foods require similar cooking temperatures and times.

6.Is it safe to leave the air fryer unattended while cooking?

It is not recommended to leave the Ninja Dual Zone Air Fryer unattended while cooking. Make sure to keep an eye on your food and check it periodically.

7.How do I cook vegetables in the air fryer?

Vegetables can be cooked in the Ninja Dual Zone Air Fryer by tossing them with a small amount of oil or seasoning and cooking at the desired temperature for 10-15 minutes, depending on the vegetable. Some vegetables may need to be blanched or par-cooked before air frying.

8.How do I preheat the air fryer?

Preheating is not necessary for all foods, but if you choose to preheat, simply turn on the air fryer and select the desired temperature. Allow the air fryer to run for a few minutes until it reaches the desired temperature before adding your food.

9.What foods can't I cook in the Ninja Dual Zone?

Not many foods can't be cooked in the Ninja Dual Zone. However, it is important to note that some delicate foods, such as soufflés or custards, may not be suitable for air frying as they require gentle and even heat. Additionally, wet batters or very moist foods may not crisp up properly in the air fryer and may result in a soggy texture.

Chapter 1: Breakfast

Devilled kidneys

Serves: 2-4
Prep Time: 10-15 minutes
Cook Time: 15-20 minutes
Ninja Dual Zone mode: Air Fry

Ingredients:
- 4 lamb kidneys, halved and deveined
- 1 tablespoon plain flour
- 1 tablespoon English mustard powder
- 1 tablespoon Worcestershire sauce
- 1 tablespoon tomato ketchup
- 1 tablespoon butter
- Salt and freshly ground black pepper
- 2 slices of toasted bread, to serve

Instructions:
1. In a small bowl, mix the flour, mustard powder, Worcestershire sauce, and tomato ketchup to make a paste.
2. Preheat the Ninja Dual Zone to Air Fry at 200°C
3. Melt the butter in a frying pan over medium heat. Add the kidneys to the pan and season with salt and pepper. Cook for 2-3 minutes on each side until browned.
4. Add the flour paste to the pan and stir well to coat the kidneys. Cook for a further 1-2 minutes until the sauce has thickened.
5. Transfer the kidneys and sauce to the Ninja Dual Zone basket and cook for 8-10 minutes until the kidneys are cooked through and the sauce is bubbling.
6. Serve the devilled kidneys on toasted bread and enjoy!

Kippers and scrambled eggs

Serves: 2
Prep Time: 5 minutes
Cook Time: 5 - 10 minutes
Ninja Dual Zone mode: Air Fry

Ingredients:
- 4 kippers
- 4 eggs
- 1 tablespoon butter
- Salt and freshly ground black pepper
- 2 slices of toasted bread, to serve

Instructions:
1. Preheat the Ninja Dual Zone to Air Fry at 190°C (190°C).
2. Place the kippers in the Ninja Dual basket and cook for 8-10 minutes until they are hot and lightly browned.
3. While the kippers are cooking, crack the eggs into a bowl and whisk together with a fork. Add salt and pepper to taste.
4. Melt the butter in a frying pan over medium heat. Add the eggs to the pan and cook, stirring gently, until they are scrambled and just set.
5. Serve the scrambled eggs with the kippers and toasted bread.

Crispy Bacon and egg pie

Serves: 4
Prep Time: 10 minutes
Cook Time: 15-20 minutes
Ninja Dual Zone mode: Bake

Ingredients:
- 1 sheet puff pastry, thawed
- 6 slices bacon, cooked until crispy and crumbled
- 4 eggs
- 118 ml of heavy cream
- Salt and freshly ground black pepper
- Chopped chives, to serve

Instructions:
1. Preheat the Ninja Dual Zone to Bake at 190°C (190°C).
2. Roll out the puff pastry on a lightly floured surface and transfer it to a 9-inch pie dish, trimming the edges as needed.
3. Sprinkle the crumbled bacon evenly over the bottom of the pie crust.
4. In a medium bowl, whisk together the eggs, heavy cream, salt, and black pepper.
5. Pour the egg mixture into the pie crust, covering the bacon.
6. Bake the pie in the Ninja Dual for 20 minutes, or until the crust is golden brown and the eggs are set.
7. Remove the pie from the Ninja Dual and let it cool for a few minutes before slicing.
8. Sprinkle with chopped chives and serve hot.

Scotch woodcock (anchovy on toast)

Serves: 2
Prep Time: 5 minutes
Cook Time: 5 minutes
Ninja Dual Zone mode: Air Fry

Ingredients:
- 4 slices of bread
- 2 tablespoons of butter
- 4-6 anchovy fillets
- 2 eggs
- Salt and freshly ground black pepper
- Chopped parsley, to serve

Instructions:
1. Preheat the Ninja Dual Zone to Air Fry at 190°C (190°C).
2. Lightly toast the bread slices and spread each slice with butter.
3. Arrange the anchovy fillets on the buttered toast.
4. Crack the eggs into a bowl and whisk together with a fork. Add salt and pepper to taste.
5. Melt the remaining butter in a frying pan over medium heat. Add the eggs to the pan and cook, stirring gently, until they are scrambled and just set.
6. Transfer the scrambled eggs to the Ninja Dual basket and cook for 1-2 minutes until hot.
7. Serve the scrambled eggs on top of the anchovy toast and sprinkle with chopped parsley.

Porridge

Serves: 4
Prep Time: 20- 25 minutes
Cook Time: 25 minutes or more
Ninja Dual Zone mode: Bake

Ingredients:
- 128g of steel-cut oats
- 750 ml of water
- 1/4 teaspoon salt
- 125 ml of milk (or non-dairy milk)
- Toppings of your choice (e.g. fresh or dried fruit, nuts, seeds, honey, maple syrup)

Instructions:
1. Rinse the steel-cut oats and place them in the Ninja Dual Zone's inner pot with water and salt.
2. Select the "Pressure Cook" function and set the timer for 10 minutes.
3. Once the timer goes off, allow the pressure to release naturally for about 10 minutes before carefully opening the lid.
4. Stir in the milk (or non-dairy milk) and mix well.
5. Serve hot in bowls and top with your desired toppings.

Full English Breakfast

Serves: 4
Prep Time: 10 minutes
Cook Time: 20 -25 minutes
Ninja Dual Zone mode: Air Fry

Ingredients:
- 4 sausages
- 4 slices of bacon
- 4 eggs
- 1 large tomato, sliced in half
- 4 mushrooms, sliced
- 1 can of baked beans
- Salt and pepper, to taste
- Olive oil or cooking spray

Instructions:
1. Preheat the Ninja Dual Zone air fryer to 190°C using the Air Fry mode.
2. Place the sausages in the air fryer basket and cook for 10 minutes, flipping halfway through.
3. Add the bacon to the air fryer basket and cook for an additional 5-7 minutes, or until crispy.
4. Remove the sausages and bacon from the air fryer and set aside on a plate.
5. Spray the air fryer basket with cooking spray or drizzle with a bit of olive oil.
6. Place the halved tomato, sliced mushrooms, and a pinch of salt and pepper in the air fryer basket.
7. Air fry the vegetables for 5-7 minutes, or until tender and slightly browned.
8. While the vegetables are cooking, heat the baked beans in a small saucepan on the stovetop.
9. Once the vegetables are done, remove them from the air fryer and set aside.
10. Crack the eggs into the air fryer basket and sprinkle with salt and pepper.
11. Air fry the eggs for 3-5 minutes, or until cooked to your liking.
12. To serve, place the sausages, bacon, eggs, tomato, mushrooms, and baked beans on a plate. Season with salt and pepper to taste.

Baked Beans

Serves: 6 Baked Beans
Prep Time: 35 - 45 minutes
Cook Time: 25 - 30 minutes
Ninja Dual Zone mode: Bake

Ingredients:

- 300g of navy beans or other white beans, drained and rinsed
- 1/2 onion, chopped
- 1/2 green pepper, chopped
- 2 cloves garlic, minced
- 125 ml ketchup
- 59 ml of molasses
- 59 ml of brown sugar
- 1 tablespoon Worcestershire sauce
- 1/2 teaspoon mustard powder
- 1/2 teaspoon smoked paprika
- 1/2 teaspoon salt
- 1/4 teaspoon black pepper
- 250 ml of water

Instructions:

1. Preheat the Ninja Dual Zone to 190°C.
2. In a mixing bowl, combine the beans, onion, green pepper, and garlic.
3. In another mixing bowl, whisk together the ketchup, molasses, brown sugar, Worcestershire sauce, mustard powder, smoked paprika, salt, and black pepper.
4. Pour the sauce over the bean mixture and stir to combine.
5. Add the bean mixture to a baking dish and add 250 ml of water.
6. Place the baking dish in the preheated Ninja Dual Zone and select the "Bake" function. Set the timer for 25-30 minutes or until the sauce is thick and bubbly.
7. Remove from the Ninja Dual Zone and serve hot.

Eggs Benedict

Serves: 4
Prep Time: 15 minutes
Cook Time: 15 minutes
Ninja Dual Zone mode: Air Fry

Ingredients:

- 4 English muffins, split and toasted
- 8 slices Canadian bacon
- 8 large eggs
- 1 tablespoon white vinegar
- Salt and pepper, to taste
- Hollandaise sauce (homemade or store-bought)
- Fresh chives, for garnish (optional)

Instructions:

1. Preheat your Ninja Dual Zone Air Fryer to 190°C
2. Arrange the Canadian bacon slices in one of the Ninja Dual sections and cook for 6-8 minutes, until browned and crispy. Transfer to a plate and cover with foil to keep warm.
3. Fill a large saucepan with water and bring to a simmer. Add the vinegar and a pinch of salt.
4. Crack one egg into a small bowl, then use a spoon to create a gentle whirlpool in the water. Carefully slide the egg into the centre of the whirlpool and cook for 2-3 minutes, until the white is set but the yolk is still runny. Use a slotted spoon to remove the egg from the water and transfer it to a plate. Repeat with the remaining eggs.
5. To assemble the Eggs Benedict, place two English muffin halves on each plate. Top each half with a slice of Canadian bacon, followed by a poached egg. Spoon hollandaise sauce over the top and sprinkle with fresh chives, if using.
6. Serve immediately and enjoy!

English Muffins

Serves: 12
Prep Time: 20 - 40 minutes
Cook Time: 20- 24 minutes
Ninja Dual Zone mode: Bake

Ingredients:

- 380g of all-purpose flour
- 59 ml of sugar
- 1 teaspoon salt
- 1 tablespoon active dry yeast
- 32g of unsalted butter, melted
- 250 ml warm milk
- 1 egg, beaten
- Cornmeal, for dusting

Instructions:

1. In a mixing bowl, combine the flour, sugar, salt, and yeast.
2. Add the melted butter, warm milk, and beaten egg. Mix until a dough forms.
3. Turn the dough out onto a lightly floured surface and knead for 10 minutes.
4. Divide the dough into 12 equal portions and shape

each portion into a ball.

5. Dust a baking sheet with cornmeal and place the dough balls on the sheet, leaving about 1 inch of space between each.

6. Dust the tops of the dough balls with more cornmeal and cover the baking sheet with a clean towel.

7. Let the dough rise in a warm place for 1 hour.

8. Preheat the Ninja Dual Zone to 177°C.

9. Remove the towel from the baking sheet and place the sheet in the preheated Ninja Dual Zone Ninja Dual .

10. Select the "Bake" function and set the timer for 10-12 minutes.

11. After the first 10-12 minutes, flip the muffins over and bake for an additional 10-12 minutes, or until they are golden brown on both sides.

12. Remove from the Ninja Dual Zone and let cool on a wire rack.

13. Once cool, use a fork to split the muffins open and toast before serving.

Scotch Pancakes

Serves: 12 Scotch Pancakes
Prep Time: 10-15 minutes
Cook Time: 10- 15 minutes
Ninja Dual Zone mode: Bake

Ingredients:
- 128g all-purpose flour
- 32g sugar
- 1 teaspoon baking powder
- 1/2 teaspoon baking soda
- 1/4 teaspoon salt
- 1 egg
- 250 ml buttermilk
- 2 tablespoons unsalted butter, melted
- 1 teaspoon vanilla extract
- Butter or oil, for cooking

Instructions:
1. In a mixing bowl, combine the flour, sugar, baking powder, baking soda, and salt.

2. In a separate bowl, beat the egg and add the buttermilk, melted butter, and vanilla extract.

3. Add the wet ingredients to the dry ingredients and mix until a smooth batter forms.

4. Preheat the Ninja Dual Zone to 190°C.

5. Lightly butter or oil a griddle or frying pan and heat over medium-high heat.

6. Using a spoon or ladle, drop the batter onto the griddle or pan to form small pancakes (about 2-3 inches in diameter).

7. Cook for 2-3 minutes, or until bubbles start to appear on the surface of the pancakes.

8. Flip the pancakes over and cook for an additional 1-2 minutes, or until golden brown.

9. Repeat with the remaining batter, adding more butter or oil to the pan as needed.

10. Serve the Scotch pancakes warm with butter, jam, or syrup.

Corned Beef Hash

Serves: 4 - 6
Prep Time: 15- 20 minutes
Cook Time: 25 -30 minutes
Ninja Dual Zone mode: Bake

Ingredients:
- 500g of cooked corned beef, chopped or shredded
- 2 large potatoes, peeled and diced
- 1 large onion, chopped
- 2 cloves garlic, minced
- 1 red bell pepper, chopped
- 2 tablespoons olive oil
- 1 tablespoon unsalted butter
- Salt and pepper, to taste
- Fresh parsley or chives, chopped (optional)

Instructions:
1. Preheat the Ninja Dual Zone to 190°C.

2. In a large bowl, mix the corned beef, potatoes, onion, garlic, and red bell pepper.

3. Drizzle the olive oil over the mixture and toss to coat evenly.

4. Season the mixture with salt and pepper to taste.

5. Melt the butter in a large skillet over medium-high heat.

6. Add the corned beef mixture to the skillet and cook for 5-7 minutes, stirring occasionally, until the potatoes are tender and the mixture is lightly browned.

7. Transfer the corned beef mixture to a baking dish or casserole dish that fits into the Ninja Dual Zone Ninja Dual .

8. Cover the dish with foil and bake for 5-7 minutes, or until the mixture is heated through.

9. Remove the foil and bake for an additional 2-3 minutes, or until the top is golden brown and crispy.

10. Sprinkle with fresh parsley or chives, if desired.

11. Serve the Corned Beef Hash hot.

Hash browns

Serves: 4
Prep Time: 10- 15 minutes
Cook Time: 20- 25 minutes
Ninja Dual Zone mode: Air Fry

Ingredients:

- 4 large potatoes, peeled and grated
- 1/2 onion, grated
- 2 tablespoons all-purpose flour
- 1 teaspoon salt
- 1/2 teaspoon freshly ground black pepper
- 59 ml of vegetable oil

Instructions:

1. Preheat the Ninja Dual Zone to Air Fry at 190°C (190°C).
2. In a large bowl, mix the grated potatoes, grated onion, flour, salt, and black pepper.
3. Pour the vegetable oil into the Ninja Dual basket and spread it evenly.
4. Spoon the potato mixture into the basket and press down lightly to form patties.
5. Cook the hash browns in the Ninja Dual for 10 minutes.
6. Carefully flip the hash browns over and cook for a further 10 minutes until golden brown and crispy.
7. Serve hot and enjoy!

Butteries

Prep Time: 15 minutes
Cook Time: 10 minutes
Servings: 8 biscuits
Ninja Dual Zone mode: Air Fry

Ingredients:

- 240g all-purpose flour
- 1 tablespoon baking powder
- 1 teaspoon salt
- 60g unsalted butter, cold and cubed
- 175ml of milk

Instructions:

1. Preheat the Ninja Dual Zone air fryer to 190°C In Airfryer mode.
2. In a large bowl, whisk together the flour, baking powder, and salt.
3. Add the cold butter cubes to the flour mixture. Use a pastry cutter or your fingers to cut the butter into the flour until the mixture resembles coarse crumbs.
4. Pour the milk into the bowl and stir until the dough comes together. Be careful not to overmix.
5. Turn the dough out onto a lightly floured surface and knead it gently a few times to bring it together.
6. Roll out the dough to about 1/2-inch thickness. Use a round biscuit cutter to cut out biscuits from the dough. Place the biscuits onto a baking sheet.
7. Open the Ninja Dual Zone air fryer and place the baking sheet with the biscuits into the lower zone.
8. Close the air fryer and set the timer for 10 minutes.
9. After 5 minutes, open the air fryer and switch the baking sheet to the upper zone for even cooking. Close the air fryer and continue cooking for the remaining 5 minutes.
10. Once the biscuits are golden brown and cooked through, remove them from the air fryer and let them cool slightly before serving.

Eggs Royale

Prep Time: 15 minutes
Cook Time: 10 minutes
Servings: 2
Ninja Dual Zone mode: Air Fry

Ingredients:

- 2 English muffins, split and toasted
- 4 slices smoked salmon
- 4 large eggs
- 2 tablespoons white vinegar
- Salt and pepper, to taste
- Hollandaise sauce:
- 3 large egg yolks
- 1 tablespoon lemon juice
- 60g unsalted butter, melted
- Salt and cayenne pepper, to taste
- Fresh dill, for garnish (optional)

Instructions:

1. Preheat the Ninja Dual Zone air fryer to 190°C In Airfryer mode.
2. In a small bowl, prepare the hollandaise sauce by whisking together the egg yolks and lemon juice until well combined.
3. Gradually pour in the melted butter while whisking continuously, until the sauce thickens. Season with salt and a pinch of cayenne pepper. Set aside.
4. Fill a large saucepan with water and add the white vinegar. Bring the water to a gentle simmer over medium heat.

5. Crack one egg into a small bowl. Create a gentle whirlpool in the simmering water using a spoon and carefully slide the egg into the center of the whirlpool. Repeat with the remaining eggs.

6. Poach the eggs for about 3-4 minutes until the whites are set and the yolks are still slightly runny. Remove the poached eggs with a slotted spoon and place them on a paper towel to drain any excess water.

7. Open the Ninja Dual Zone air fryer and place the toasted English muffin halves in the lower zone.

8. Close the air fryer and set the timer for 2 minutes to warm up the muffins.

9. After 2 minutes, open the air fryer and place a slice of smoked salmon on each English muffin half. Place a poached egg on top of the salmon.

10. Close the air fryer and set the timer for an additional 2 minutes to warm up the salmon and eggs.

11. Once the salmon and eggs are warmed through, remove the English muffins from the air fryer.

12. Drizzle hollandaise sauce generously over each Eggs Royale. Season with salt, pepper, and garnish with fresh dill if desired.

13. Serve the Eggs Royale immediately while still warm.

Shropshire Fidget Pie

Prep Time: 30 minutes
Cook Time: 40 minutes
Servings: 4
Ninja Dual Zone mode: Air Dry and Bake
Ingredients:
- 400g puff pastry
- 1 tablespoon olive oil
- 1 onion, chopped
- 2 cloves of garlic, minced
- 200g bacon, chopped
- 2 large potatoes, peeled and cubed
- 2 apples, peeled, cored, and sliced
- 200ml vegetable broth
- 1 teaspoon dried thyme
- Salt and pepper, to taste
- 1 egg, beaten (for egg wash)

Instructions:

1. Preheat the Ninja Dual Zone air fryer to 180°C in Zone 1 for air frying.

2. In a large pan, heat the olive oil over medium heat. Add the chopped onion and minced garlic, and sauté until softened and lightly golden.

3. Add the chopped bacon to the pan and cook until crispy. Remove the bacon and set aside, leaving the rendered fat in the pan.

4. In the same pan with the bacon fat, add the cubed potatoes and sliced apples. Cook for a few minutes until they start to soften slightly.

5. Add the vegetable broth, dried thyme, salt, and pepper to the pan. Stir well and bring to a simmer. Cook for about 5 minutes or until the potatoes are just tender. Remove from heat and let the filling mixture cool slightly.

6. Roll out the puff pastry on a lightly floured surface to fit the base and top of your pie dish. Line the base of the pie dish with one sheet of puff pastry.

7. Fill the pie dish with the slightly cooled potato and apple mixture, then sprinkle the cooked bacon evenly over the top.

8. Cover the filling with the second sheet of puff pastry. Press the edges to seal and trim off any excess pastry. Cut a few slits on the top to allow steam to escape during baking.

9. Brush the top of the pastry with beaten egg to give it a golden shine.

10. Place the pie dish in the Ninja Dual Zone air fryer in Zone 2 for baking. Bake at 180°C for approximately 30-40 minutes or until the pastry is golden brown and crispy.

11. Once cooked, remove the Shropshire Fidget Pie from the Ninja Dual Zone air fryer and let it cool slightly before serving.

12. Serve the Shropshire Fidget Pie warm as a main course, accompanied by a side of vegetables or a green salad.

Eggs in Purgatory

Prep Time: 10 minutes
Cook Time: 20 minutes
Servings: 2
Ninja Dual Zone mode: Air Fry
Ingredients:
- 2 tablespoons olive oil
- 1/2 onion, finely chopped
- 2 cloves garlic, minced
- 1/2 teaspoon red pepper flakes (adjust to taste)
- 1 can crushed tomatoes
- 1/2 teaspoon dried oregano
- 1/2 teaspoon dried basil
- Salt and pepper, to taste

- 4 large eggs
- Fresh basil or parsley, chopped (for garnish)
- Grated Parmesan cheese (optional, for serving)
- Crusty bread (for serving)

Instructions:

1. Preheat the Ninja Dual Zone air fryer to 190°C in Air Fry mode.
2. In a skillet or frying pan, heat the olive oil over medium heat. Add the chopped onion and sauté until it becomes translucent, about 3-4 minutes.
3. Add the minced garlic and red pepper flakes to the skillet, and sauté for an additional 1 minute.
4. Stir in the crushed tomatoes, dried oregano, dried basil, salt, and pepper. Let the sauce simmer for about 10 minutes, until it thickens slightly.
5. Open the Ninja Dual Zone air fryer and pour the tomato sauce into the lower zone. Close the air fryer and set the timer for 5 minutes to warm up the sauce.
6. After 5 minutes, open the air fryer and carefully crack the eggs into the tomato sauce, making sure to space them evenly. Season the eggs with a sprinkle of salt and pepper.
7. Close the air fryer and set the timer for an additional 10 minutes to cook the eggs. Check the eggs occasionally and cook them to your desired level of doneness (runny yolks or fully cooked).
8. Once the eggs are cooked to your liking, remove the skillet from the air fryer.
9. Garnish the Eggs in Purgatory with freshly chopped basil or parsley. If desired, sprinkle grated Parmesan cheese on top.
10. Serve the Eggs in Purgatory directly from the skillet with some crusty bread for dipping.

Staffordshire Oatcakes

Prep Time: 15 minutes
Cook Time: 20 minutes
Servings: 4 oatcakes
Ninja Dual Zone mode: Air Fry

Ingredients:

- 80g oats (rolled or quick oats)
- 125g all-purpose flour
- 1/2 teaspoon salt
- 1 teaspoon baking powder
- 250ml of milk
- Butter or oil, for cooking

- Optional fillings: cooked bacon, cheese, mushrooms, etc.

Instructions:

1. Preheat the Ninja Dual Zone air fryer to 190°C in Air Fry mode.
2. In a large mixing bowl, combine the oats, flour, salt, and baking powder. Mix well to combine.
3. Gradually add the milk to the dry ingredients, stirring continuously, until you have a smooth batter. The consistency should be similar to pancake batter. Let the batter rest for 10 minutes to allow the oats to soften.
4. Open the Ninja Dual Zone air fryer and place a non-stick frying pan or skillet in the lower zone. Add a small amount of butter or oil to the pan and let it heat up.
5. Pour approximately 60g of batter into the hot pan, swirling it around to form a thin, round oatcake. Cook for 2-3 minutes, until the edges start to brown and the oatcake is set.
6. Carefully flip the oatcake using a spatula and cook for an additional 2-3 minutes on the other side. Repeat this process with the remaining batter to make more oatcakes.
7. As each oatcake is cooked, transfer it to the upper zone of the air fryer to keep warm while you cook the others.
8. Once all the oatcakes are cooked, you can fill them with your desired ingredients, such as cooked bacon, cheese, mushrooms, or any other toppings of your choice.
9. Fold the oatcakes in half to enclose the fillings, or roll them up like a wrap.
10. Place the filled oatcakes back into the air fryer for 1-2 minutes to warm through.
11. Remove the oatcakes from the air fryer and serve them warm.

Crispy Bacon and Tomato Sandwich

Prep Time: 5 minutes
Cook Time: 15 minutes
Servings: 2 sandwiches
Ninja Dual Zone mode: Air Fry

Ingredients:

- 8 slices bacon
- 4 slices bread (white, whole wheat, or your preference)
- 4 lettuce leaves

- 4 tomato slices
- Mayonnaise or your favourite sandwich spread
- Salt and pepper, to taste

Instructions:
1. Preheat the Ninja Dual Zone air fryer to 200°C in Air Fry mode.
2. Lay the bacon slices in a single layer in the lower zone of the air fryer. Close the air fryer and set the timer for 12-15 minutes, or until the bacon is crispy to your liking.
3. While the bacon is cooking, prepare the other ingredients. Wash and dry the lettuce leaves, and slice the tomatoes. Set them aside.
4. Open the air fryer and check the bacon. If it's not crispy enough, close the air fryer and cook for an additional 1-2 minutes, as needed.
5. Once the bacon is cooked to your desired crispiness, remove it from the air fryer and place it on a paper towel-lined plate to drain any excess grease.
6. Place the bread slices in the upper zone of the air fryer. Close the air fryer and set the timer for 2 minutes to lightly toast the bread.
7. After 2 minutes, open the air fryer and remove the bread slices.
8. Spread mayonnaise or your preferred sandwich spread on one side of each bread slice.
9. Layer the crispy bacon slices, lettuce leaves, and tomato slices onto two slices of bread. Sprinkle with salt and pepper to taste.
10. Top the sandwich fillings with the remaining bread slices, spread side down.
11. If desired, cut the sandwiches in half diagonally or into smaller portions.

Bacon and Cheese Scones

Prep Time: 15 minutes
Cook Time: 12 minutes
Servings: 8 scones
Ninja Dual Zone mode: Air Fry

Ingredients:
- 240g of all-purpose flour
- 1 tablespoon baking powder
- 1/2 teaspoon salt
- 59ml unsalted butter, cold and cubed
- 250ml grated cheddar cheese
- 60g cooked bacon, crumbled
- 175ml milk
- 1 egg, beaten (for egg wash)

Instructions:
1. Preheat the Ninja Dual Zone air fryer to 190°C in Air Fry mode.
2. In a large bowl, whisk together the flour, baking powder, and salt.
3. Add the cold cubed butter to the flour mixture. Use a pastry cutter or your fingers to cut the butter into the flour until the mixture resembles coarse crumbs.
4. Stir in the grated cheddar cheese and crumbled bacon into the flour mixture.
5. Pour the milk into the bowl and stir until the dough comes together. Be careful not to overmix.
6. Turn the dough out onto a lightly floured surface and knead it gently a few times to bring it together.
7. Roll out the dough to about 1-inch thickness. Use a round biscuit cutter or a glass to cut out scones from the dough. Place the scones onto a baking sheet lined with parchment paper.
8. Brush the tops of the scones with the beaten egg to create a shiny glaze.
9. Open the Ninja Dual Zone air fryer and place the baking sheet with the scones into the lower zone.
10. Close the air fryer and set the timer for 12 minutes.
11. After 6 minutes, open the air fryer and switch the baking sheet to the upper zone for even cooking. Close the air fryer and continue cooking for the remaining 6 minutes.
12. Once the scones are golden brown and cooked through, remove them from the air fryer and let them cool slightly before serving.

Irish Soda Bread

Prep Time: 10 minutes
Cook Time: 20 minutes
Servings: 1 loaf
Ninja Dual Zone mode: Air Fry

Ingredients:
- 500g all-purpose flour
- 1 teaspoon baking soda
- 1 teaspoon salt
- 414ml buttermilk
- Optional: 1 tablespoon honey or sugar
- Optional: 125ml raisins or currants

Instructions:
1. Preheat the Ninja Dual Zone air fryer to 190°C in Air Fry mode.
2. In a large mixing bowl, whisk together the flour,

baking soda, and salt.

3. If desired, add honey or sugar to the dry ingredients and mix well. This will add a touch of sweetness to the bread.

4. If using raisins or currants, add them to the dry ingredients and toss them to coat with flour. This will prevent them from sinking to the bottom of the bread.

5. Make a well in the center of the dry ingredients and pour in the buttermilk. Use a wooden spoon or your hands to mix the ingredients until a dough forms. It may be slightly sticky.

6. Turn the dough out onto a lightly floured surface and knead it gently a few times to bring it together.

7. Shape the dough into a round loaf and place it on a baking sheet lined with parchment paper.

8. Use a sharp knife to score a shallow "X" on the top of the loaf. This helps the bread bake evenly.

9. Open the Ninja Dual Zone air fryer and place the baking sheet with the dough into the lower zone.

10. Close the air fryer and set the timer for 20 minutes to bake the bread.

11. After 10 minutes, open the air fryer and rotate the baking sheet to ensure even browning. Close the air fryer and continue baking for the remaining 10 minutes.

12. Once the bread is golden brown and sounds hollow when tapped on the bottom, remove it from the air fryer and let it cool on a wire rack.

13. Slice and serve the Irish Soda Bread. It is delicious on its own, or you can spread it with butter or your favourite jam.

Cumbrian Fellbred Sausage and Tomato Casserole

Prep Time: 15 minutes
Cook Time: 40 minutes
Servings: 4
Ninja Dual Zone mode: Bake
Ingredients:
- 500g (1.1 lb) Cumbrian Fellbred sausages (or any other high-quality sausage of your choice)
- 1 tablespoon olive oil
- 1 onion, diced
- 2 cloves of garlic, minced
- 2 carrots, peeled and sliced
- 2 celery stalks, sliced

- 1 can (400g/14 oz) chopped tomatoes
- 1 tablespoon tomato paste
- 250ml beef or vegetable broth
- 1 teaspoon dried thyme
- 1 teaspoon dried rosemary
- Salt and pepper, to taste
- Fresh parsley, chopped (for garnish)

Instructions:
1. Preheat the Ninja Dual Zone air fryer to 200°C in Zone 1 for searing/sautéing.

2. In Zone 1 of the Ninja Dual Zone, heat the olive oil. Add the sausages and brown them on all sides. This should take about 5 minutes. Once browned, remove the sausages from the air fryer and set aside.

3. In the same Zone 1 of the Ninja Dual Zone, add the diced onion, minced garlic, sliced carrots, and celery. Sauté until the vegetables are slightly softened and the onion becomes translucent.

4. Transfer the sautéed vegetables to Zone 2 of the Ninja Dual Zone (slow cook setting).

5. Add the browned sausages back into Zone 2 with the vegetables.

6. To Zone 2, add the chopped tomatoes, tomato paste, beef or vegetable broth, dried thyme, dried rosemary, salt, and pepper. Stir everything together to combine.

7. Close the Ninja Dual Zone and set the slow cook function to 140°C for 40 minutes. This will allow the flavours to meld together and the sausages to cook through.

8. After 40 minutes, carefully open the Ninja Dual Zone and check that the sausages are cooked through. Adjust the seasoning if needed.

9. Serve the Cumbrian Fellbred Sausage and Tomato Casserole hot, garnished with freshly chopped parsley.

10. This casserole pairs well with mashed potatoes, rice, or crusty bread.

Banana and Nutella Pancakes

Prep Time: 10 minutes
Cook Time: 15 minutes
Servings: 4 pancakes
Ninja Dual Zone mode: Air Fry
Ingredients:
- 125g of all-purpose flour
- 2 tablespoons granulated sugar
- 1 teaspoon baking powder

- 1/2 teaspoon baking soda
- 1/4 teaspoon salt
- 240g of buttermilk
- 1 large egg
- 2 tablespoons unsalted butter, melted
- 1 ripe banana, mashed
- Nutella, for spreading
- Sliced bananas, for topping (optional)
- Chopped nuts, for topping (optional)

Instructions:

1. Preheat the Ninja Dual Zone air fryer to 190°C in Air Fry mode.
2. In a large bowl, whisk together the flour, sugar, baking powder, baking soda, and salt.
3. In a separate bowl, whisk together the buttermilk, egg, melted butter, and mashed banana.
4. Pour the wet ingredients into the dry ingredients and stir until just combined. Be careful not to overmix; a few lumps in the batter are fine.
5. Open the Ninja Dual Zone air fryer and place a non-stick frying pan or skillet in the lower zone. Add a small amount of butter or oil to the pan and let it heat up.
6. Pour approximately 55g of pancake batter into the hot pan for each pancake. Cook for about 2 minutes, until bubbles form on the surface.
7. Carefully flip the pancake using a spatula and cook for an additional 1-2 minutes on the other side, until golden brown.
8. Transfer the cooked pancake to the upper zone of the air fryer to keep warm while you cook the remaining pancakes.
9. Repeat the process with the remaining batter to make more pancakes.
10. Once all the pancakes are cooked, spread Nutella on each pancake.
11. Stack the Nutella-spread pancakes on a serving plate.
12. Top the pancakes with sliced bananas and chopped nuts, if desired.

Vegetarian Breakfast Hash

Prep Time: 15 minutes
Cook Time: 25 minutes
Servings: 4
Ninja Dual Zone mode: Air Fry

Ingredients:

- 2 tablespoons olive oil
- 1 small onion, diced
- 2 cloves garlic, minced
- 2 medium potatoes, peeled and diced
- 1 red bell pepper, diced
- 1 green bell pepper, diced
- 1 zucchini, diced
- 75g of sliced mushrooms
- 1 teaspoon paprika
- 1/2 teaspoon dried thyme
- 1/2 teaspoon dried oregano
- Salt and pepper, to taste
- Optional toppings: chopped fresh herbs (such as parsley or chives), shredded cheese, hot sauce

Instructions:

1. Preheat the Ninja Dual Zone air fryer to 200°C in Air Fry mode.
2. In a large skillet, heat the olive oil over medium heat. Add the diced onion and minced garlic, and sauté until the onion becomes translucent and fragrant.
3. Add the diced potatoes to the skillet and cook for 5-7 minutes, stirring occasionally, until the potatoes start to soften.
4. Add the diced red and green bell peppers, zucchini, and sliced mushrooms to the skillet. Continue cooking for another 5 minutes, until the vegetables are tender.
5. Sprinkle the paprika, dried thyme, dried oregano, salt, and pepper over the vegetables. Stir well to coat the vegetables evenly with the spices.
6. Transfer the seasoned vegetable mixture to the lower zone of the Ninja Dual Zone air fryer. Close the air fryer and set the timer for 20 minutes.
7. After 10 minutes, open the air fryer and stir the vegetables to ensure even cooking. Close the air fryer and continue cooking for the remaining 10 minutes.
8. While the vegetables are cooking, prepare any desired toppings, such as chopped fresh herbs, shredded cheese, or hot sauce.
9. Once the breakfast hash is cooked and the vegetables are nicely browned and crispy, remove the skillet from the air fryer.
10. Serve the Vegetarian Breakfast Hash hot, topped with any desired toppings.

Welsh Glamorgan Sausages

Prep Time: 15 minutes
Cook Time: 15 minutes
Servings: 4
Ninja Dual Zone Settings: Air Fry

Ingredients:

- 200g Caerphilly cheese, grated
- 100g fresh breadcrumbs
- 1 tablespoon chopped fresh parsley
- 1 tablespoon chopped fresh thyme
- 1 teaspoon mustard powder
- 2 cloves of garlic, minced
- 2 large eggs
- 100ml milk
- Salt and pepper, to taste
- 50g all-purpose flour
- Olive oil (for brushing)

Instructions:

1. Preheat the Ninja Dual Zone air fryer to 200°C in Zone 1 for air frying.
2. In a large mixing bowl, combine the grated Caerphilly cheese, fresh breadcrumbs, chopped parsley, chopped thyme, mustard powder, minced garlic, salt, and pepper. Mix well.
3. In a separate bowl, whisk together the eggs and milk. Pour the egg mixture over the cheese and breadcrumb mixture. Stir everything together until well combined. The mixture should be moist but firm enough to shape into sausages.
4. Divide the mixture into 8 equal portions and shape each portion into a sausage shape.
5. Place the all-purpose flour on a plate and roll each sausage in the flour, coating all sides.
6. Place the coated sausages in Zone 1 of the Ninja Dual Zone air fryer. Brush them lightly with olive oil to promote browning.
7. Close the Ninja Dual Zone and air fry the Glamorgan sausages at 200°C for approximately 12-15 minutes, or until they are golden brown and crispy on the outside.
8. While the sausages are air frying, preheat Zone 2 of the Ninja Dual Zone to bake mode.
9. Once the sausages are cooked, transfer them to Zone 2 of the Ninja Dual Zone to keep warm while you finish cooking any remaining batches.
10. Serve the Welsh Glamorgan Sausages hot as a main course or as a vegetarian alternative for

traditional sausages. They pair well with mashed potatoes and a side of vegetables or a fresh salad.

Smoked Mackerel Pâté

Prep Time: 10 minutes
Cook Time: 0 minutes (No cooking required)
Servings: 4
Ninja Dual Zone mode: Air Fry

Ingredients:

- 2 smoked mackerel fillets, skin removed
- 113g of cream cheese
- 2 tablespoons Greek yoghourt
- 1 tablespoon lemon juice
- 1 tablespoon chopped fresh dill
- Salt and pepper, to taste
- Optional: Toasted bread or crackers for serving

Instructions:

1. In a bowl, break up the smoked mackerel fillets into small flakes using a fork.
2. In a separate bowl, combine the cream cheese, Greek yoghourt, lemon juice, and chopped fresh dill. Stir until well mixed.
3. Add the flaked smoked mackerel to the cream cheese mixture. Stir gently to combine, ensuring the fish is evenly distributed.
4. Season the pâté with salt and pepper to taste. Adjust the seasoning as desired.
5. Transfer the Smoked Mackerel Pâté to a serving dish.
6. If using the Ninja Dual Zone air fryer for other components of your meal, you can use the air fryer to toast bread or crackers to serve alongside the pâté. Simply place the bread or crackers in the air fryer and toast them for a few minutes until crispy and golden.
7. Serve the Smoked Mackerel Pâté with toasted bread or crackers.

Variety Pop Tarts

Prep Time: 4 minutes
Cook Time: 4 minutes
Servings: 8
Ninja Dual Zone mode: Roast

Ingredients

- 2 Chocolate pop tarts
- 2 Strawberry pop tarts
- 2 Apple pop tarts
- 2 Cherry pop tarts

Instructions:

1. Preheat the dual zone at 200°C with the crisper plate
2. Place 4 pop tarts in each zone draw of the air fryer
3. Pair the zone draws to 'ROAST' at 200°C for 4 minutes
4. Press 'MATCH' followed by 'STOP/START' to toast the pop tarts
5. Flip the pop tarts at the 2 minute mark of cooking
6. After they pop tarts are cooked, retrieve them and plate them up to be served

Sweet Porridge Duo

Prep Time: 5 minutes
Cook Time: 6 minutes
Servings: 4
Ninja Dual Zone mode: Bake

Ingredients

- 240g porridge oats
- 500ml milk or water
- 1 tbsp brown sugar
- 30g Marmalade
- 30g honey
- 40g flaxseed

Instructions:

1. Pour the oats, milk, raisins, and sugar into a mixing bowl and stir thoroughly
2. Pour the oats mixture 2 oven proof bowls
3. Select the zones, followed by 'BAKE' at 180°C for 10 minutes
4. Press 'MATCH' and 'STOP/START' to initiate the baking process
5. Retrieve the oats and divide them into 4 bowls
6. Top 2 bowls with marmalade and 20g of flaxseed and the other 2 bowls with honey and 20g flaxseed
7. Stir the porridge thoroughly before serving

Egg in a Hole

Prep Time: 10 minutes
Cook Time: 10 minutes
Servings: 4
Ninja Dual Zone mode: Bake

Ingredients

- 4 thick slices of wholemeal bread
- 20g butter
- 4 small eggs
- 1/4 tsp red pepper flakes, crushed
- Sea salt and ground black pepper, to taste

Instructions:

1. Spread butter on the bread slices. Push the middle of the bread down to form a well (you can use a small mug). Repeat with the remaining bread slices.
2. Crack an egg into each well; season with salt, red pepper, and black pepper.
3. Add the bread slices to lightly-greased drawers.
4. Select zone 1 and pair it with "BAKE" at 165°C for 10 minutes. Select "MATCH" followed by the "START/STOP" button.

Hot Sandwiches

Prep Time: 5 minutes
Cook Time: 22 minutes
Servings: 5
Ninja Dual Zone mode: Air Fry and Roast

Ingredients

- 200g Canadian bacon, uncooked
- 500g courgette, cut into 2.5cm slices
- Sea salt and ground black pepper, to taste
- 1/4 tsp cayenne pepper, or more to taste
- 1 tbsp olive oil
- 1 large tomato, sliced
- 1 tbsp English mustard
- 5 medium sandwich buns

Instructions:

1. Insert a crisping plate in both drawers. Add bacon to the zone 1 drawer.
2. Toss the courgette with salt, black pepper, cayenne pepper, and olive oil until the slices are well coated on all sides. Put the courgette slices into the zone 2 drawer.
3. Select zone 1 and pair it with "AIR FRY" at 180°C for 10 minutes. Select zone 2 and pair it with "ROAST" at 200°C for 18 minutes. Select "SYNC" followed by the "START/STOP" button.
4. Divide the bacon, courgette, tomato, and mustard among the sandwich buns.
5. Now, arrange the assembled sandwiches in both drawers in your Ninja Foodi. Select "REHEAT" at 170°C for 4 minutes.

Crunchy Granola

Prep Time: 5 minutes
Cook Time: 15 minutes
Servings: 8
Ninja Dual Zone mode: Roast

Ingredients

- 200g rolled oats
- 100g walnuts, roughly chopped
- 50g coconut oil
- 100g honey
- 80g pumpkin seeds
- 30g hemp seeds
- 50g walnuts, roughly chopped
- 1/2 tsp ground cloves
- 1 tsp ground cinnamon

Instructions:

1. Begin by preheating your Ninja Foodi to 180°C. Line two roasting tins that fit in your Ninja Foodi with baking paper.
2. Mix the oats, walnuts, coconut oil, and 50g of honey. Spread the mixture onto a roasting tin and add the roasting tin to the zone 1 drawer.
3. Mix the remaining Ingredients, spread the mixture onto a roasting tin and add it to the zone 2 drawer.
4. Select zone 1 and pair it with "ROAST" at 170°C for 15 minutes. Select zone 2 and pair it with "ROAST" at 170°C for 9 minutes. Select "SYNC" followed by the "START/STOP" button.
5. When zone 1 time reaches 8 minutes, stir the Ingredients, and reinsert the drawer to continue cooking.
6. When zone 2 time reaches 5 minutes, stir the Ingredients, and reinsert the drawer to continue cooking.
7. Add the oat/nut mixture to the seed mixture and stir to combine well; let your granola cool before serving and storing. Enjoy!

Omelette with Spinach and Peppers

Prep Time: 10 minutes
Cook Time: 13 minutes
Servings: 4
Ninja Dual Zone mode: Bake

Ingredients

- 7 whole eggs
- 100g double cream
- 1 medium onion, peeled and chopped
- 1 medium bell pepper, deseeded and chopped
- 60g baby spinach
- Sea salt and ground black pepper, to taste

Instructions:

1. Remove a crisper plate from your Nina Foodi. Very lightly butter two baking tins.
2. In a mixing bowl, thoroughly combine all the Ingredients.
3. Spoon the mixture into the prepared baking tins. Place the tins in the prepared drawers.
4. Select zone 1 and pair it with "BAKE" at 180°C for 13 minutes. Select "MATCH" followed by the "START/STOP" button.

Easy Frittata

Prep Time: 10 minutes
Cook Time: 13 minutes
Servings: 4
Ninja Dual Zone mode: Bake

Ingredients

- 8 whole eggs
- 100g double cream
- 2 spring onions, thinly sliced
- 1 tsp curry paste
- 300g tomatoes, halved
- 1 red chilli pepper, deseeded and minced
- 1/2 tsp garlic granules
- Sea salt and ground black pepper, to taste

Instructions:

1. Remove a crisper plate from your Nina Foodi. Spray drawers with cooking oil; now, line the base with a sheet of parchment paper.
2. Preheat the Ninja Foodi to 180°C for 5 minutes.
3. In a mixing bowl, thoroughly combine all the Ingredients. Spoon the frittata mixture into the prepared drawers.
4. Select zone 1 and pair it with "BAKE" at 180°C for 13 minutes. Select "MATCH" followed by the "START/STOP" button.

Chapter 2: Lunch

Grilled Chicken Fajitas

Serves: 4
Prep Time: 10 minutes
Cook Time: 20 minutes
Ninja Dual Zone mode: Air Fry

Ingredients:

- 500 g of boneless, skinless chicken breasts, sliced into thin strips
- 2 bell peppers, sliced into thin strips
- 1 onion, sliced into thin strips
- 2 tbsp olive oil
- 2 tbsp taco seasoning
- Salt and pepper, to taste
- Flour or corn tortillas
- Optional toppings: shredded cheese, sour cream, guacamole, salsa

Instructions:

1. Preheat the Ninja Dual Zone to Air Fry mode at 190°C for 5 minutes.
2. In a large bowl, toss the chicken strips with 1 tbsp of olive oil and taco seasoning until evenly coated.
3. Place the chicken strips in the basket of the Ninja Dual Zone and cook for 8-10 minutes, or until cooked through, flipping halfway through.
4. Remove the chicken from the basket and set aside.
5. In the same bowl, toss the sliced peppers and onions with the remaining 1 tbsp of olive oil, salt, and pepper.
6. Place the pepper and onion mixture in the basket of the Ninja Dual Zone and cook for 6-8 minutes, or until they are tender and slightly charred, stirring halfway through.
7. Add the cooked chicken back to the basket and toss everything together to combine.
8. Serve the fajita mixture with warm tortillas and any desired toppings.

Spinach and Feta Stuffed Chicken

Serves: 4
Prep Time: 15 minutes
Cook Time: 18-20 minutes
Ninja Dual Zone mode: Air Fry

Ingredients:

- 4 boneless, skinless chicken breasts
- 250 ml of fresh spinach leaves, chopped
- 125 ml of crumbled feta cheese
- 2 tablespoons olive oil
- 1 teaspoon garlic powder
- 1/2 teaspoon onion powder
- 1/2 teaspoon dried basil
- Salt and pepper, to taste

Instructions:

1. Preheat your Ninja Dual Zone to Air Fry mode at 190°C.
2. In a bowl, mix the chopped spinach, crumbled feta cheese, olive oil, garlic powder, onion powder, dried basil, salt, and pepper.
3. Cut a pocket into each chicken breast by slicing horizontally through the thickest part, but not all the way through.
4. Stuff each chicken breast with the spinach and feta mixture, then use toothpicks to secure the opening.
5. Place the stuffed chicken breasts in the Vortex Plus Ninja Dual basket and air fry for 18-20 minutes, flipping halfway through, until the chicken is cooked through and golden brown.
6. Remove the toothpicks from the chicken and serve hot.

Vietnamese Banh Mi Sandwiches

Serves: 4
Prep Time: 20 minutes
Cook Time: 15 minutes
Ninja Dual Zone mode: Air Fry

Ingredients:
- 4 French baguettes
- 500 g of boneless pork shoulder, sliced thinly
- 2 tbsp. vegetable oil
- 2 cloves garlic, minced
- 1 tbsp. soy sauce
- 1 tbsp. fish sauce
- 1 tbsp. brown sugar
- 1/2 tsp. black pepper
- 64g of mayonnaise
- 1 tbsp. sriracha sauce
- 1 tbsp. lime juice
- 1 tsp. sugar
- 1/2 tsp. salt
- 125 ml of pickled carrots and daikon radish
- 59 ml of chopped fresh cilantro
- 1 jalapeno, sliced
- 4 lettuce leaves

Instructions:
1. Preheat Ninja Dual Zone to Air Fry at 200°C.
2. In a large bowl, combine pork, vegetable oil, garlic, soy sauce, fish sauce, brown sugar, and black pepper. Toss to coat.
3. Place pork in the Ninja Dual Zone and air fry for 12-15 minutes, or until the pork is cooked through and crispy.
4. While the pork is cooking, prepare the sauce by combining mayonnaise, sriracha sauce, lime juice, sugar, and salt in a small bowl. Set aside.
5. Cut the baguettes in half and toast them in the Ninja Dual Zone for 2-3 minutes.
6. Spread the sauce on both sides of the baguette.
7. Add the pickled carrots and daikon radish, chopped cilantro, jalapeno, and lettuce to the sandwich.
8. Add the crispy pork to the sandwich and serve.

Quiche Lorraine

Serves: 6
Prep Time: 15 minutes
Cook Time: 30-35 minutes
Ninja Dual Zone mode: Bake

Ingredients:
- 1 store-bought pie crust
- 6 large eggs
- 190g of heavy cream
- 250 ml of shredded Gruyere or Swiss cheese
- 6 slices bacon, cooked and crumbled
- 1/2 small onion, finely chopped
- 1/4 teaspoon salt
- 1/4 teaspoon black pepper
- 1/8 teaspoon ground nutmeg

Instructions:
1. Preheat the Ninja Dual Zone to Bake mode at 190°C.
2. Roll out the pie crust and fit it into a 9-inch pie dish. Trim the excess crust and crimp the edges.
3. In a medium bowl, whisk together the eggs, heavy cream, salt, pepper, and nutmeg until well combined.
4. Sprinkle the shredded cheese, cooked bacon, and chopped onion evenly over the bottom of the pie crust.
5. Pour the egg mixture over the filling Ingredients in the pie crust, ensuring they are evenly covered.
6. Place the quiche in the Ninja Dual Zone and bake for 30-35 minutes, or until the centre is set and the top is golden brown.
7. Remove the quiche from the Ninja Dual Zone and let it cool for a few minutes before slicing and serving.

Falafel

Serves: 4
Prep Time: 15 minutes
Cook Time: 15-20 minutes
Ninja Dual Zone mode: Air Fry

Ingredients:
- 122 g of dried chickpeas
- 122 g of chopped onion
- 64g fresh parsley leaves
- 64g fresh cilantro leaves
- 2 cloves garlic, minced
- 1 tablespoon flour
- 1 teaspoon baking powder
- 1 1/2 teaspoons ground cumin
- 1 teaspoon ground coriander
- 1/4 teaspoon cayenne pepper
- 1 teaspoon salt
- Oil spray

Instructions:

1. Soak chickpeas in water for at least 12 hours, or overnight. Drain and rinse well.
2. In a food processor, pulse chickpeas until they resemble coarse sand. Add in onion, parsley, cilantro, and garlic, and pulse until finely chopped and mixed with the chickpeas.
3. Transfer the mixture to a large mixing bowl. Add in flour, baking powder, cumin, coriander, cayenne pepper, and salt. Mix well.
4. Preheat the Ninja Dual Zone to air fry at 190°C.
5. Form mixture into small balls, about the size of a golf ball. Spray the basket of the Ninja Dual Zone with oil spray, and place falafel balls in the basket, making sure they are not touching.
6. Air fry falafel for 10 minutes. Open the basket and use tongs to flip the falafel. Air fry for another 5-10 minutes until they are crispy and golden brown.
7. Serve hot with pita bread, hummus, and tzatziki sauce.

Pulled Pork Sandwiches

Serves: 6-8
Prep Time: 10 minutes
Cook Time: 1 hour 30 minutes (plus time for the Ninja Dual Zone to reach pressure)
Ninja Dual Zone mode: Bake

Ingredients:

- 1500 to 2000 g of pork shoulder
- 1 tbsp. smoked paprika
- 1 tbsp. garlic powder
- 1 tbsp. onion powder
- 1 tbsp. brown sugar
- 1 tsp. salt
- 1/2 tsp. black pepper
- 125 ml apple cider vinegar
- 125 ml ketchup
- 32g brown sugar
- 2 tbsp. Dijon mustard
- 2 tbsp. Worcestershire sauce
- 2 tbsp. honey
- 1 tbsp. smoked paprika
- 1 tbsp. garlic powder
- 1/2 tsp. salt
- 1/2 tsp. black pepper
- 250 ml of water

For serving:

- Buns or rolls
- Coleslaw

Instructions:

1. In a small bowl, mix the smoked paprika, garlic powder, onion powder, brown sugar, salt, and black pepper. Rub the mixture all over the pork shoulder.
2. In a separate bowl, whisk together the apple cider vinegar, ketchup, brown sugar, Dijon mustard, Worcestershire sauce, honey, smoked paprika, garlic powder, salt, black pepper, and water.
3. Pour the sauce into the Ninja Dual Zone cooking pot.
4. Add the seasoned pork shoulder to the cooking pot and spoon some of the sauce on top.
5. Close the lid and set the Ninja Dual Zone to Pressure Cook mode for 1 hour and 30 minutes.
6. Once the cooking time is up, release the pressure manually and carefully remove the pork shoulder from the cooking pot.
7. Using two forks, shred the pork and mix it with the remaining sauce in the pot.
8. Serve the pulled pork on buns or rolls with coleslaw.

Welsh Cawl

Serves: 4-6
Prep Time: 20 minutes
Cook Time: 1 hour
Ninja Dual Zone modes: Roast and Bake

Ingredients:

- 1000 g of lamb or beef, cut into bite-sized pieces
- 2 tbsp vegetable oil
- 1 onion, chopped
- 3 garlic cloves, minced
- 3 carrots, chopped
- 2 leeks, sliced
- 2 turnips, chopped
- 1 tbsp chopped fresh thyme
- 1 tbsp chopped fresh rosemary
- 1440 g of beef broth
- Salt and pepper, to taste

Instructions:

1. Set your Ninja Dual Zone to Roast mode and preheat it to 190°C.
2. Heat the vegetable oil in a large pan over medium-high heat. Add the lamb or beef and cook until browned on all sides, about 5-7 minutes.

3. Add the chopped onion, garlic, carrots, leeks, and turnips to the pan and cook for another 5 minutes until the vegetables are slightly softened.
4. Transfer the meat and vegetables to the Ninja Dual Zone basket. Add the thyme, rosemary, beef broth, and season with salt and pepper.
5. Set the Ninja Dual Zone to Slow Cook mode and cook for 1 hour, stirring occasionally.
6. Serve hot with a slice of crusty bread and enjoy!

Quesadillas

Serve: 2-4
Prep Time: 10 minutes
Cook Time: 6-8 minutes
Ninja Dual Zone mode: Air Fry

Ingredients:
- 4 large flour tortillas
- 256g of shredded cheese (cheddar, Monterey Jack, or a combination)
- 64g of cooked chicken or beef, diced (optional)
- 64g of diced bell pepper
- 64g diced onion
- 64g salsa
- 32g chopped fresh cilantro

Instructions:
1. Preheat the Ninja Dual Zone to Air Fry at 190°C.
2. Lay one flour tortilla flat and sprinkle half of the shredded cheese on top.
3. Add the cooked chicken or beef, if using, followed by the bell pepper, onion, and salsa.
4. Sprinkle the remaining cheese and cilantro over the top.
5. Place another tortilla on top of the Ingredients and press down slightly.
6. Carefully place the quesadilla in the Ninja Dual Zone basket and cook for 6-8 minutes, or until the cheese is melted and the tortilla is crispy.
7. Remove from the basket using tongs and let cool for 1-2 minutes.
8. Cut into wedges and serve with additional salsa and sour cream, if desired.

Tuna Melt

Here's a recipe for Tuna Melt using the Ninja Dual Zone Ninja Dual :

Serves: 2
Prep Time: 10 minutes
Cook Time: 10-15 minutes

Ninja Dual Zone mode: Bake
Ingredients:
- 1 can of tuna, drained
- 32g mayonnaise
- 32g celery, finely diced
- 32g red onion, finely diced
- 1 tablespoon lemon juice
- 1/2 teaspoon black pepper
- 4 slices of bread
- 4 slices of cheddar cheese
- Butter

Instructions:
1. Preheat your Ninja Dual Zone to the Bake mode at 177°C (175°C).
2. In a mixing bowl, combine the tuna, mayonnaise, celery, red onion, lemon juice, and black pepper. Mix until everything is well combined.
3. Butter one side of each slice of bread.
4. Place two slices of bread butter-side down onto a baking sheet.
5. Place a slice of cheese on each slice of bread, and then divide the tuna mixture between the two slices of bread.
6. Place another slice of cheese on top of the tuna mixture, and then place the remaining slices of bread on top, butter-side up.
7. Place the baking sheet into the preheated Ninja Dual Zone and bake for 10-12 minutes, or until the cheese is melted and the bread is golden brown.
8. Remove from the oven and allow to cool for a few minutes before serving.

Shrimp Po'Boys

Serves: 4
Prep Time: 15 minutes
Cook Time: 10 minutes
Ninja Dual Zone mode: Air Fry

Ingredients:
- 500 g large shrimp, peeled and deveined
- 128g all-purpose flour
- 1 teaspoon paprika
- 1/2 teaspoon garlic powder
- 1/2 teaspoon onion powder
- 1/2 teaspoon cayenne pepper
- Salt and pepper to taste
- 128g buttermilk

- 120g seasoned bread crumbs
- 4 hoagie rolls
- 64g mayonnaise
- 2 tablespoons chopped fresh parsley
- 2 tablespoons fresh lemon juice
- 2 garlic cloves, minced
- Lettuce, tomato, and pickles for serving

Instructions:

1. In a bowl, mix the flour, paprika, garlic powder, onion powder, cayenne pepper, salt, and pepper.
2. Pour the buttermilk into another bowl.
3. In a third bowl, mix the bread crumbs and a pinch of salt.
4. Coat the shrimp in the flour mixture, then dip them in the buttermilk, and finally coat them in the bread crumbs.
5. Place the shrimp in the Ninja Dual Zone basket and air fry at 200°C for 8-10 minutes or until they are golden brown and cooked through.
6. While the shrimp are cooking, mix the mayonnaise, parsley, lemon juice, and garlic.
7. To assemble the po' boys, spread the garlic mayo on the hoagie rolls, add lettuce and tomato slices, top with the cooked shrimp, and add pickles if desired.
8. Serve and enjoy your delicious Shrimp Po'Boys!

Corn and Bacon Chowder

Serves: 4-6
Prep Time: 15 minutes
Cook Time: 25 minutes
Ninja Dual Zone mode:
Bake

Ingredients:

- 6 slices bacon, diced
- 1 onion, diced
- 3 cloves garlic, minced
- 2 potatoes, peeled and diced
- 256g of frozen corn kernels
- 256g of chicken or vegetable broth
- 250 ml milk
- 128g of heavy cream
- Salt and pepper, to taste
- Fresh chives or green onions, chopped (optional)

Instructions:

1. Preheat your Ninja Dual Zone to Bake mode at 190°C.

2. In a large pot or Dutch oven, cook the diced bacon until crispy. Remove the bacon with a slotted spoon and set aside, leaving the bacon grease in the pot.
3. Add the diced onion and minced garlic to the pot and sauté until the onion is translucent, about 5 minutes.
4. Add the diced potatoes, frozen corn, and chicken or vegetable broth to the pot. Bring to a boil, then reduce heat and simmer for 10-15 minutes, or until the potatoes are tender.
5. Add the milk and heavy cream to the pot and stir to combine. Let simmer for 5-10 more minutes.
6. Season with salt and pepper to taste.
7. Serve hot, garnished with crispy bacon and chopped chives or green onions (if using).

Mushroom and Stilton Quiche

Prep Time: 20 minutes
Cook Time: 35 minutes
Servings: 6-8
Ninja Dual Zone mode: Air Fry

Ingredients:

- 1 pre-made pie crust
- 1 tablespoon olive oil
- 220g of mushrooms, sliced
- 1 small onion, finely chopped
- 3 cloves garlic, minced
- 4 large eggs
- 240g of heavy cream
- 55g of crumbled Stilton cheese (or any other blue cheese)
- Salt and pepper, to taste
- Fresh thyme leaves, for garnish (optional)

Instructions:

1. Preheat the Ninja Dual Zone air fryer to 190°C in Air Fry mode.
2. Roll out the pre-made pie crust and line a 9-inch pie dish with it. Trim any excess crust hanging over the edges.
3. In a skillet, heat the olive oil over medium heat. Add the sliced mushrooms, chopped onion, and minced garlic. Sauté until the mushrooms have softened and released their moisture, and the onion is translucent. Remove from heat and let cool slightly.
4. In a mixing bowl, whisk together the eggs and

heavy cream. Season with salt and pepper to taste.

5. Spread the sautéed mushroom mixture evenly over the bottom of the pie crust.

6. Pour the egg and cream mixture over the mushrooms, ensuring they are well coated.

7. Sprinkle the crumbled Stilton cheese evenly over the top of the quiche.

8. Open the Ninja Dual Zone air fryer and place the pie dish into the lower zone. Close the air fryer and set the timer for 35 minutes to bake the quiche.

9. After 20 minutes, open the air fryer and rotate the pie dish to ensure even browning. Close the air fryer and continue baking for the remaining 15 minutes, or until the quiche is set and golden brown on top.

10. Once the quiche is cooked, carefully remove it from the air fryer and let it cool for a few minutes.

11. Garnish with fresh thyme leaves, if desired.

Caprese Sandwich

Prep Time: 10 minutes
Cook Time: 5 minutes
Servings: 2
Ninja Dual Zone mode: Air Fry
Ingredients:

• 4 slices of bread (preferably ciabatta or baguette)
• 2 tablespoons extra virgin olive oil
• 2 large tomatoes, sliced
• 200g fresh mozzarella cheese, sliced
• Handful of fresh basil leaves
• Balsamic glaze, for drizzling
• Salt and pepper, to taste

Instructions:

1. Preheat the Ninja Dual Zone air fryer to 180°C in Air Fry mode

2. Brush one side of each bread slice with extra virgin olive oil.

3. In the Ninja Dual Zone, place the bread slices with the oiled side down. Air fry for about 2-3 minutes or until the bread is toasted and golden brown.

4. While the bread is toasting, assemble the sandwich by layering tomato slices, mozzarella slices, and fresh basil leaves on the untoasted side of two bread slices.

5. Season the tomato and mozzarella layers with salt and pepper to taste.

6. Drizzle balsamic glaze over the tomato and mozzarella layers.

7. Once the bread slices are toasted, place the assembled sandwiches in the Ninja Dual Zone for toasting. Toast for about 2 minutes or until the mozzarella cheese starts to melt.

8. Carefully remove the Caprese Sandwiches from the Ninja Dual Zone and let them cool slightly.

9. Cut the sandwiches in half and serve them warm.

Tomato and Basil Bruschetta

Prep Time: 10 minutes
Cook Time: 5 minutes
Servings: 4-6
Ninja Dual Zone mode: Air Fry
Ingredients:

• 1 French baguette, sliced into 1/2-inch thick slices
• 4-5 ripe tomatoes, diced
• 10g fresh basil leaves, chopped
• 2 cloves garlic, minced
• 2 tablespoons extra-virgin olive oil
• 1 tablespoon balsamic vinegar
• Salt and pepper, to taste

Instructions:

1. Preheat the Ninja Dual Zone air fryer to 200°C in Air Fry mode.

2. Arrange the baguette slices on a baking sheet and brush them lightly with olive oil.

3. Open the air fryer and place the baking sheet with the baguette slices in the lower zone. Close the air fryer and set the timer for 5 minutes to toast the bread slices.

4. In a bowl, combine the diced tomatoes, chopped basil, minced garlic, olive oil, and balsamic vinegar. Toss gently to mix well.

5. Season the tomato mixture with salt and pepper to taste. Adjust the seasoning as desired.

6. Once the baguette slices are toasted and crispy, remove them from the air fryer and let them cool for a minute or two.

7. Spoon the tomato and basil mixture onto each baguette slice, spreading it evenly.

8. Serve the Tomato and Basil Bruschetta immediately as an appetizer or a light snack.

Coronation Chicken Salad

Prep Time: 15 minutes
Cook Time: 25 minutes
Servings: 4-6
Ninja Dual Zone mode: Air Fry

Ingredients:
- 240g cooked chicken breast, diced or shredded
- 120g mayonnaise
- 60g Greek yoghourt
- 2 tablespoons mango chutney
- 1 tablespoon curry powder
- 1 tablespoon lemon juice
- 40g raisins or sultanas
- 30g slivered almonds
- Salt and pepper, to taste
- Optional: Fresh cilantro or parsley for garnish

Instructions:
1. Preheat the Ninja Dual Zone air fryer to 190°C in Air Fry mode.
2. If you don't have cooked chicken breast, you can cook it in the air fryer. Season the chicken breast with salt and pepper, then place it in the lower zone of the air fryer. Close the air fryer and cook for 20-25 minutes, or until the chicken is cooked through. Remove from the air fryer and let it cool before dicing or shredding.
3. In a mixing bowl, combine the mayonnaise, Greek yogurt, mango chutney, curry powder, lemon juice, raisins or sultanas, and slivered almonds. Stir until well combined.
4. Add the diced or shredded cooked chicken to the dressing mixture. Mix well to coat the chicken evenly with the dressing.
5. Season with salt and pepper to taste. Adjust the seasoning and flavours according to your preference.
6. Open the Ninja Dual Zone air fryer and place the chicken salad in the lower zone. Close the air fryer and set the timer for 5 minutes to chill and let the flavours meld.
7. Once the chicken salad is chilled, remove it from the air fryer.
8. Garnish the Coronation Chicken Salad with fresh cilantro or parsley, if desired.

Ham and Cheese Toasties

Prep Time: 10 minutes
Cook Time: 5 minutes

Servings: 2
Ninja Dual Zone mode: Air Fry

Ingredients:
- 4 slices of bread
- Butter, softened
- 4-6 slices of ham
- 4 slices of cheese (such as cheddar, Swiss, or Gouda)
- Optional: Mustard or mayonnaise for spreading

Instructions:
1. Preheat the Ninja Dual Zone air fryer to 190°C in Air Fry mode.
2. Spread a thin layer of softened butter on one side of each bread slice.
3. If desired, spread mustard or mayonnaise on the other side of the bread slices.
4. Place 1-2 slices of ham on two of the bread slices, ensuring they cover the buttered side.
5. Top the ham with 2 slices of cheese on each bread slice.
6. Place the remaining bread slices on top of the cheese, with the buttered side facing out.
7. Open the Ninja Dual Zone air fryer and place the assembled ham and cheese toasties in the lower zone.
8. Close the air fryer and set the timer for 5 minutes to toast the sandwiches.
9. After 2-3 minutes, open the air fryer and flip the toasties using a spatula to ensure even browning. Close the air fryer and continue cooking for the remaining time, or until the sandwiches are golden brown and the cheese is melted.
10. Once the toasties are cooked, carefully remove them from the air fryer and let them cool for a minute before serving.

Tandoori Vegetable Skewers

Prep Time: 20 minutes
Marinating time: 1-2 hours
Cook Time: 12-15 minutes
Servings: 4-6
Ninja Dual Zone mode: Air Fry

Ingredients:
- 1 large red bell pepper, cut into chunks
- 1 large yellow bell pepper, cut into chunks
- 1 large green bell pepper, cut into chunks
- 1 medium red onion, cut into chunks

- 1 medium zucchini, sliced into thick rounds
- 1 medium eggplant, cut into chunks
- 240ml plain Greek yoghourt
- 2 tablespoons tandoori masala powder
- 2 tablespoons lemon juice
- 2 tablespoons olive oil
- 2 cloves garlic, minced
- 1 teaspoon ground cumin
- 1 teaspoon ground coriander
- 1/2 teaspoon turmeric powder
- 1/2 teaspoon paprika
- Salt and pepper, to taste
- Optional: Fresh cilantro for garnish

Instructions:
1. Preheat the Ninja Dual Zone air fryer to 200°C in Air Fry mode.
2. In a bowl, combine the Greek yogurt, tandoori masala powder, lemon juice, olive oil, minced garlic, ground cumin, ground coriander, turmeric powder, paprika, salt, and pepper. Mix well to make the marinade.
3. Add the bell peppers, red onion, zucchini, and eggplant to the marinade. Toss gently to coat the vegetables evenly with the marinade. Let the vegetables marinate in the refrigerator for 1-2 hours to allow the flavours to develop.
4. Thread the marinated vegetables onto skewers, alternating the different vegetables.
5. Open the Ninja Dual Zone air fryer and place the vegetable skewers in the lower zone. Close the air fryer and set the timer for 12-15 minutes to cook the skewers.
6. After 6-7 minutes, open the air fryer and flip the skewers using tongs for even cooking. Close the air fryer and continue cooking for the remaining time, or until the vegetables are tender and slightly charred.
7. Once the vegetable skewers are cooked to your liking, remove them from the air fryer and let them cool for a minute.
8. Garnish with fresh cilantro, if desired.

Tuna Nicoise Salad

Prep Time: 15 minutes
Cook Time: 10 minutes
Servings: 2
Ninja Dual Zone mode: Air Fry

Ingredients:
- 2 eggs
- 200g green beans, trimmed
- 200g cherry tomatoes, halved
- 1 small red onion, thinly sliced
- 12 Kalamata olives
- 2 cans of tuna, drained
- 4 small potatoes, boiled and quartered
- Handful of fresh basil leaves
- Handful of fresh parsley leaves
- 2 tablespoons extra virgin olive oil
- 2 tablespoons red wine vinegar
- Salt and pepper, to taste

Instructions:
1. Preheat the Ninja Dual Zone air fryer to 200°C in Air Fry mode.
2. Place the eggs in Zone 1 of the Ninja Dual Zone. Air fry them for about 10 minutes, or until they reach your desired level of doneness (typically hard-boiled). Once cooked, remove the eggs from the air fryer and let them cool. Peel and quarter the eggs.
3. In the meantime, in Zone 1 of the Ninja Dual Zone, place the trimmed green beans. Air fry them for about 5-7 minutes, or until they are tender-crisp. Once cooked, remove the green beans from the air fryer and let them cool.
4. In a large bowl, combine the halved cherry tomatoes, sliced red onion, Kalamata olives, drained tuna, quartered boiled potatoes, cooked green beans, fresh basil leaves, and fresh parsley leaves.
5. In a small bowl, whisk together the extra virgin olive oil, red wine vinegar, salt, and pepper to make the dressing.
6. Drizzle the dressing over the salad mixture in the large bowl. Toss gently to combine, ensuring all Ingredients are coated with the dressing.
7. Divide the salad into individual plates or bowls.
8. Top each plate with the quartered hard-boiled eggs.
9. Serve the Tuna Nicoise Salad immediately and enjoy as a light and satisfying meal.

Stuffed Portobello Mushrooms

Prep Time: 15 minutes
Cook Time: 12-15 minutes
Servings: 4
Ninja Dual Zone mode: Air Fry

Ingredients:
- 4 large Portobello mushrooms
- 1 tablespoon olive oil
- 1 small onion, finely chopped
- 2 cloves garlic, minced
- 60g breadcrumbs
- 50g grated Parmesan cheese
- 10g chopped fresh parsley
- 30g chopped sun-dried tomatoes
- 1/4 teaspoon dried oregano
- Salt and pepper, to taste
- Optional: Additional grated Parmesan cheese for topping

Instructions:
1. Preheat the Ninja Dual Zone air fryer to 190°C in Air Fry mode.
2. Clean the Portobello mushrooms and remove the stems. Gently scrape out the gills using a spoon to create more space for the stuffing.
3. In a skillet, heat the olive oil over medium heat. Add the chopped onion and minced garlic and sauté until the onion is translucent and fragrant.
4. In a bowl, combine the sautéed onion and garlic mixture with the breadcrumbs, grated Parmesan cheese, chopped parsley, sun-dried tomatoes, dried oregano, salt, and pepper. Mix well to form the stuffing mixture.
5. Spoon the stuffing mixture into the cavity of each Portobello mushroom, pressing it down gently to fill the mushrooms completely.
6. Open the Ninja Dual Zone air fryer and place the stuffed Portobello mushrooms in the lower zone. Close the air fryer and set the timer for 12-15 minutes to cook the mushrooms.
7. After 6-7 minutes, open the air fryer and sprinkle additional grated Parmesan cheese on top of each mushroom, if desired. Close the air fryer and continue cooking for the remaining time, or until the mushrooms are tender and the stuffing is golden brown.
8. Once the stuffed Portobello mushrooms are cooked to your liking, remove them from the air fryer and let them cool for a minute before serving.

20 Steak Sandwich

Prep Time: 15 minutes
Cook Time: 10-12 minutes
Servings: 2
Ninja Dual Zone mode: Air Fry

Ingredients:
- 2 steak fillets (such as ribeye or sirloin), about 6-8 ounces each
- Salt and pepper, to taste
- 2 tablespoons olive oil
- 1 small onion, thinly sliced
- 1 bell pepper, thinly sliced
- 4 slices of provolone or Swiss cheese
- 2 bread rolls or baguettes, sliced
- Optional: Mayonnaise, mustard, or other desired condiments

Instructions:
1. Preheat the Ninja Dual Zone air fryer to 200°C in Air Fry mode.
2. Season the steak fillets with salt and pepper on both sides.
3. Open the air fryer and place the seasoned steak fillets in the lower zone. Close the air fryer and set the timer for 6-8 minutes for medium-rare doneness. Adjust the cooking time based on your desired level of doneness.
4. While the steak is cooking, heat the olive oil in a skillet over medium heat. Add the sliced onion and bell pepper and sauté until they are soft and caramelized.
5. Once the steak is cooked to your liking, remove it from the air fryer and let it rest for a few minutes. Slice the steak into thin strips against the grain.
6. Open the air fryer and place the sliced bread rolls or baguettes in the lower zone. Close the air fryer and set the timer for 2-3 minutes to warm and slightly toast the bread.
7. Assemble the steak sandwiches by spreading desired condiments, such as mayonnaise or mustard, on the bread slices. Layer the sliced steak, sautéed onions and bell peppers, and slices of provolone or Swiss cheese.
8. Open the air fryer and place the assembled sandwiches in the lower zone. Close the air fryer and set the timer for 2-3 minutes to melt the cheese and warm the sandwich.
9. Once the cheese has melted and the sandwich is

warmed through, remove it from the air fryer and let it cool for a minute before serving.

Hot Sea Scallop and Pepper Salad

Prep Time: 10 minutes
Cook Time: 12 minutes
Servings: 4
Ninja Dual Zone mode: Air Fry

Ingredients

- 600g sea scallops
- 1 small knob of fresh root ginger, peeled and grated
- 1 tsp mustard seeds
- 1 large garlic clove, peeled
- 1 rosemary sprig, leaves picked
- 1 thyme sprig, leaves picked
- Sea salt and ground black pepper, to taste
- 1 medium lemon, freshly squeezed
- 2 tbsp extra-virgin olive oil
- 600g bell peppers, deveined and sliced
- 1 red chilli pepper, deveined and sliced
- 2 scallion stalks, chopped
- 1 head Romaine lettuce

Instructions:

1. Insert crisper plates in both drawers and spray them with cooking oil. Pat the sea scallops dry with paper towels.
2. Crush the ginger, mustard seeds, garlic, rosemary, and thyme using a pestle and mortar. Then, add salt, black pepper, 1 tablespoon of olive oil, and lemon juice; mix to combine well.
3. Rub the scallops with the spice/lemon mixture. Toss bell peppers with 1 tablespoon of olive oil, salt, black pepper, and red chilli pepper.
4. Add the scallops to the zone 1 drawer and the bell peppers to the zone 2 drawer.
5. Select zone 1 and pair it with "AIR FRY" at 200°C for 8 minutes. Select zone 2 and pair it with "AIR FRY" at 200°C for 12 minutes. Select "SYNC" followed by the "START/STOP" button.
6. Shake the drawers halfway through the cooking time. Toss your scallops with roasted bell peppers, scallions, and lettuce. Enjoy!

Air Fried Shrimp & Pasta

Prep Time: 5 minutes
Cook Time: 13 minutes
Servings: 8
Ninja Dual Zone mode: Air Fry

Ingredients

- 1kg Shrimp
- 250ml olive oil
- 60ml lemon juice
- 2 tsp black pepper, grounded
- 1 tsp Sea salt
- 550g pasta, cooked

Instructions:

1. Preheat the dual zone to 200° for 5 minutes with the crisper plates
2. In the meantime, hand amalgamate all of the Ingredients in a medium sized mixing bowl
3. Divide the shrimp amongst both zone draws and pair them to 'AIR FRY' at 200°C for 10 minutes
4. Press 'MATCH' followed by 'START/STOP' to initiate the air frying process
5. At the 5 minute mark of air frying, give the shrimp a shake
6. During the last 5 minutes of cooking, plate up 8 portions of pasta
7. Once done, retrieve the shrimp and divide them on top of each pasta plates to serve

Tandoori Haddock Burger

Prep Time: 20 minutes
Cook Time: 10 minutes
Servings: 2
Ninja Dual Zone mode: Air Fry and Roast

Ingredients

- 25g tandoori masala
- 50ml flaxseed oil
- 55g Greek yogurt
- 2 x 150g Haddock fillets
- 2 sliced pickles
- 2 slices of red onion
- 2 Brioche Buns, halved
- 1/8 tbsp Himalayan salt
- 1/8 tbsp white pepper, grounded

Instructions:

1. Preheat the air fryer at 180°C for 5 minutes
2. Using a mixing bowl, combine ¾ of the olive oil, all of the tandoori masala, 1/3 of the Greek

yogurt, and salt using a fork

3. Dip the Haddock pieces into this mixture and coat well
4. Use the rest of the oil to grease bottom part of the zone 1 draw
5. Place the Haddock zone 1 draw and the buns in the zone 2 draw
6. Pair the zone 1 draw to 'AIR FRY' at 180°C for 10 minutes, and the buns in the zone 2 draw to 'ROAST' at 170° for 2 minutes
7. Press 'MATCH' followed by 'START/STOP' to cook the fish and heat the buns
8. Retrieve the food content and place red onion on the bottom layer of the bun, then top this with tandoori haddock, pickle and the upper layer of the bun
9. Plate these burgers up to serve

Authentic Ratatouille

Prep Time: 10 minutes
Cook Time: 15 minutes
Servings: 4
Ninja Dual Zone mode: Bake

Ingredients

- 2 medium courgettes, sliced
- 1 medium tomato, diced
- 4 bell peppers, seeded and sliced
- 2 medium aubergine, sliced
- 3 garlic cloves, chopped
- 1 medium onion, sliced
- 2 tsp olive oil
- 1 tbsp Herb de Provence
- 300 ml tomato sauce

Instructions:

1. Toss the vegetables with olive oil and Herb de Provence. Arrange the vegetables in an alternating pattern in lightly-greased drawers.
2. Spoon the tomato sauce over the vegetables.
3. Select zone 1 and pair it with "BAKE" at 190°C for 15 minutes. Select "MATCH" to duplicate settings across both zones. Press the "START/ STOP" button.

Vegetable Medley

Prep Time: 5 minutes
Cook Time: 20 minutes
Servings: 4
Ninja Dual Zone mode: Bake

Ingredients

- 650g courgettes, medium diced
- 400g aubergine, medium diced
- 2 bell peppers, seeded and sliced
- 1 medium onion, peeled and sliced
- 2 tbsp olive oil
- 1 tbsp thyme
- 1 tbsp rosemary
- 1 tbsp cayenne pepper
- Sea salt and ground black pepper, to taste
- 120g mozzarella cheese, sliced

Instructions:

1. Thoroughly combine the vegetables with olive oil and spices. Divide the medley mixture between two baking tins.
2. Add baking tins to the drawers.
3. Select zone 1 and pair it with "BAKE" at 180°C for 20 minutes. Select "MATCH" to duplicate settings across both zones. Press the "START/ STOP" button.
4. When zone 1 time reaches 10 minutes, top each medley with cheese; reinsert the drawer to continue cooking.

Roasted Beetroot and Carrot Salad

Prep Time: 10 minutes
Cook Time: 45 minutes
Servings: 4
Ninja Dual Zone mode: Roast

Ingredients

- 1 kg small beetroots, whole
- 500g carrots, peeled, cut into 1.5cm pieces
- 1 tbsp olive oil
- 2 tbsp apple cider vinegar
- 1 orange, freshly squeezed
- 2 tbsp extra-virgin olive oil
- 1 small chilli pepper, seeded and chopped
- 2 tbsp pumpkin seeds
- 80g pomegranate seeds
- A few sprigs of fresh parsley, chopped
- 100g goat cheese, room temperature, crumbled

Instructions:

1. Place beetroots in the zone 1 drawer. Toss the carrots with 1 tablespoon of olive oil and transfer them to the zone 2 drawer.
2. Select zone 1 and pair it with "ROAST" at 200°C for 40 to 45 minutes. Select zone 2 and

pair it with "ROAST" at 200°C for 16 minutes. Select "SYNC" followed by the "START/STOP" button.

3. At the halfway point, shake your food or toss it with silicone-tipped tongs to promote even cooking. Reinsert the drawer to continue cooking.

4. Toss beetroots and carrots with the remaining Ingredients. Serve your salad at room temperature or well-chilled.

Bacon Snack With Worchester Sauce

Prep Time: 2 minutes
Cook Time: 10 minutes
Servings: 4
Ninja Dual Zone mode: Air Fry

Ingredients
- 24 Bacon streaky rashers
- 2 tbsp Bacon flavour bits
- 60ml Worchester sauce
- 1 cal avocado fry spray

Instructions:
1. Spray the zone draws of the ninja foodi, then preheat the ninja foodi to 200°C for 5 minutes
2. Toss 12 bacon rashers into the ninja zone drawl and sprinkle the Bacon flavour bits on top
3. Set the zones to be paired with 'AIR FRY' setting on the ninja air fryer at 200°C for 10 minutes
4. Press 'MATCH' followed by 'STOP/START' air fry the bacon
5. At the 4 minute mark of cooking, pull out the zone draws and pour in Worchester sauce and give the bacon rashers a shake
6. At the end of the cooking duration, retrieve the bacon snack then serve

Simple Clams

Prep Time: 5 minutes
Cook Time: 15 minutes
Servings: 8
Ninja Dual Zone mode: Bake

Ingredients
- 1 packet of clams

Instructions:
1. Preheat the dual zone to 190°C for 5 minutes
2. Toss the clams in both draws of the dual zone

3. Pair the zone draws to 'BAKE' at 190°C for 7minutes, then press 'MATCH' and 'START/STOP' to cook the clams
4. At the 4 minute mark of cooking, give the clams a shake
5. Once cooked, retrieve the clams and serve

Nutty Millet Bake

Prep Time: 10 minutes
Cook Time: 28 minutes
Servings: 5
Ninja Dual Zone mode: Bake

Ingredients
- 2 tsp butter, melted
- 350g millet, rinsed
- 1 litre milk
- 100g prunes, pitted and chopped
- 2 eggs, beaten
- 120g almonds, chopped
- 1/2 tsp vanilla bean paste
- 1/2 tsp ground cinnamon
- 1/2 tsp grated nutmeg (optional)

Instructions:
1. Remove a crisper plate from your Ninja Foodi. Brush two oven-safe baking tins with the melted butter.
2. Tip the millet into a deep saucepan and pour in the milk; add 350ml of water and bring it to a boil. Reduce the heat to medium-low; leave to simmer for 13 to 15 minutes, stirring continuously, until the millet is tender.
3. Mix the millet with the other Ingredients and spoon the mixture into the prepared baking tins. Add the baking tins to the drawers.
4. Select zone 1 and pair it with "BAKE" at 180°C for 13 minutes. Select "MATCH" to duplicate settings across both zones. Press the "START/STOP" button.
5. When zone 1 time reaches 6 minutes, rotate both baking tins and reinsert the drawers to continue cooking.

Chapter 3: Dinner

Steak Diane

Serves: 2
Prep Time: 10 minutes
Cook Time: 10- 15 minutes
Ninja Dual Zone mode: Air Fry

Ingredients:
- 2 beef tenderloin steaks, about 8 oz each
- 1 tablespoon olive oil
- 2 tablespoons unsalted butter
- 32g finely chopped shallots
- 32g beef stock
- 2 tablespoons Worcestershire sauce
- 2 tablespoons Dijon mustard
- 32g heavy cream
- Salt and pepper, to taste
- Chopped parsley, for garnish

Instructions:
1. Preheat the Ninja Dual Zone to Sear at 200°C (200°C).
2. Season the beef tenderloin steaks with salt and pepper on both sides.
3. Add the olive oil to the Ninja Dual and sear the steaks for 2-3 minutes on each side, or until well browned and cooked to your desired level of doneness.
4. Remove the steaks from the Ninja Dual and set them aside on a plate.
5. In the same pan, add the butter and shallots and cook for 1-2 minutes, or until softened.
6. Add the beef stock, Worcestershire sauce, and Dijon mustard to the pan and stir to combine.
7. Cook the sauce for 1-2 minutes, or until slightly reduced.
8. Add the heavy cream to the pan and cook for another minute, stirring constantly.
9. Season the sauce with salt and pepper to taste.
10. Return the cooked steaks to the pan and spoon the sauce over them.
11. Garnish the Steak Diane with chopped parsley and serve immediately.

Fish and Chips

Serves: 4-6
Prep Time: 20 minutes
Cook Time: 12-15 minutes
Ninja Dual Zone mode: Air Fry

Ingredients:
- 4-6 white fish fillets (such as cod or haddock)
- 128g all-purpose flour
- 1 tsp salt
- 1/2 tsp black pepper
- 1/2 tsp garlic powder
- 1/2 tsp paprika
- 1/4 tsp cayenne pepper
- 250 ml of beer
- 1 large egg
- 4-6 large potatoes, cut into thick chips
- 2 tbsp olive oil
- Salt and pepper, to taste

Instructions:
1. Preheat your Ninja Dual Zone to Air Fry mode at 190°C (190°C).
2. In a large bowl, whisk together the flour, salt, black pepper, garlic powder, paprika, and cayenne pepper.
3. In a separate bowl, whisk together the beer and egg.
4. Dip each fish fillet into the beer mixture, then into the flour mixture, making sure to coat evenly.
5. Place the coated fish fillets onto the Air Fryer basket, making sure to leave some space in between.
6. In another bowl, toss the potato chips with the olive oil and salt and pepper to taste.
7. Place the potato chips in the Air Fryer basket next to the fish fillets.
8. Cook for 12-15 minutes, flipping the fish fillets and potato chips halfway through, until the fish is golden brown and cooked through, and the potato chips are crispy.
9. Serve hot with tartar sauce, lemon wedges, and your favourite sides.

Roast Pork Belly

Serves: 4-6
Prep Time: 10 minutes
Cook Time: 50-60 minutes
Ninja Dual Zone mode: Air Fry and Roast
Ingredients:
- 1000 g pork belly, skin-on
- 1 tablespoon salt
- 1 tablespoon black pepper
- 1 tablespoon garlic powder

- 1 tablespoon onion powder
- 1 tablespoon dried thyme
- 1 tablespoon paprika

Instructions:

1. Preheat the Ninja Dual Zone air fryer to 190°C (190°C) using the Ninja Dual feature.
2. In a small bowl, mix the salt, black pepper, garlic powder, onion powder, dried thyme, and paprika.
3. Score the skin of the pork belly in a cross-hatch pattern using a sharp knife.
4. Rub the spice mixture all over the pork belly, making sure to get into the scored skin.
5. Place the pork belly, skin side up, into the air fryer basket with the Ninja Dual set to "Roast" for 45 minutes.
6. After 45 minutes, remove the pork belly from the air fryer and let it rest for 10 minutes.
7. Turn the Ninja Dual to "Air Fryer" and place the pork belly back in the air fryer for an additional 5-10 minutes to crisp up the skin.
8. Remove the pork belly from the air fryer and let it rest for an additional 10 minutes before slicing and serving.

Stew and Dumplings

Serves: 4-6
Prep Time: 20 minutes
Cook Time: 50 minutes
Ninja Dual Zone mode: Air Fry

Ingredients:

- 1000 g beef stew meat, cut into 1-inch pieces
- 2 tablespoons all-purpose flour
- 2 tablespoons olive oil
- 1 onion, chopped
- 3 garlic cloves, minced
- 540 g of beef broth
- 256g of chopped carrots
- 256g of chopped celery
- 1 teaspoon dried thyme
- 1 bay leaf
- Salt and pepper to taste
- 128g all-purpose flour
- 2 teaspoons baking powder
- 1/2 teaspoon salt
- 64g milk
- 2 tablespoons butter, melted

Instructions:

1. In a large bowl, toss the beef stew meat with 2

tablespoons of flour until coated.
2. Set the Ninja Dual Zone to Air Fry mode and preheat to 190°C.
3. Add the olive oil to the inner pot and wait for it to get hot.
4. Add the coated beef to the pot and cook until browned on all sides, about 5 minutes.
5. Add the chopped onion and garlic and cook for another 2-3 minutes.
6. Pour in the beef broth and add the chopped carrots, celery, thyme, bay leaf, salt, and pepper.
7. stir everything and close the lid.
8. Set the Ninja Dual Zone to Stew mode and cook for 30 minutes.
9. While the stew is cooking, make the dumplings. In a medium bowl, mix the flour, baking powder, and salt.
10. Add the milk and melted butter and mix until just combined.
11. Once the stew has finished cooking, open the lid and drop spoonfuls of the dumpling batter onto the surface of the stew.
12. Close the lid and set the Ninja Dual Zone to Air Fry mode at 190°C. Cook for another 15-20 minutes or until the dumplings are cooked through and golden brown.
13. Serve the stew and dumplings hot and enjoy!

Roast Beef with Yorkshire Pudding

Serves: 6-8
Prep Time: 10 minutes
Cook Time: 1 hour 15 minutes
Ninja Dual Zone mode: Air Fry

Ingredients:

- 408 g beef roast
- Salt and pepper to taste
- 1 tbsp olive oil
- 1 onion, sliced
- 3 garlic cloves, minced
- 128g beef broth
- 125 ml of red wine
- 1 tbsp Worcestershire sauce
- 1 tsp dried thyme
- 1/2 tsp dried rosemary
- 2 tbsp butter
- 2 tbsp all-purpose flour
- 170 g of milk
- 2 eggs
- 128g all-purpose flour

- 1/2 tsp salt
- 250 ml of vegetable oil

Instructions:
1. Preheat the Ninja Dual Zone to Air Fry mode at 190°C.
2. Season the beef roast with salt and pepper.
3. Heat the olive oil in a large skillet over medium-high heat. Add the beef and sear on all sides until browned, about 4-5 minutes per side.
4. Transfer the beef to the Ninja Dual Zone basket and place it in the Air Fryer.
5. In the same skillet, add the sliced onions and garlic and cook until tender, about 3-4 minutes.
6. Add the beef broth, red wine, Worcestershire sauce, thyme, and rosemary to the skillet and stir to combine.
7. Pour the mixture over the beef in the Air Fryer basket.
8. Air Fry for 50-60 minutes or until the beef is cooked to your desired level of doneness.
9. In a separate bowl, whisk together the flour, milk, and eggs until smooth.
10. Add the salt and continue to whisk until the mixture is well combined.
11. Heat the vegetable oil in a 9-inch baking dish until hot.
12. Pour the batter into the baking dish and bake in the Air Fryer at 190°C for 20-25 minutes, or until the Yorkshire pudding is puffed and golden brown.
13. In a small saucepan, melt the butter over medium heat. Add the flour and whisk until smooth.
14. Gradually add the beef broth mixture from the Air Fryer to the saucepan, whisking constantly, until the gravy thickens.
15. Serve the roast beef with the Yorkshire pudding and gravy on the side. Enjoy!

Cottage Pie

Serves: 6
Prep Time: 15 minutes
Cook Time: 25 minutes
Ninja Dual Zone mode: Bake
Ingredients:
- 500 g ground beef
- 1 onion, diced
- 2 cloves garlic, minced
- 2 medium carrots, diced
- 1 tbsp tomato paste
- 1 tbsp Worcestershire sauce
- 128g beef broth

- 2 tbsp cornstarch
- 1 tsp dried thyme
- 1 tsp dried rosemary
- Salt and pepper, to taste
- 408 g of mashed potatoes
- 64g shredded cheddar cheese

Instructions:
1. Preheat the Ninja Dual Zone to the bake mode at 190°C.
2. In a large skillet, cook the ground beef over medium-high heat until browned, stirring occasionally. Drain any excess fat.
3. Add the onion, garlic, and carrots to the skillet and sauté until the vegetables are tender, about 5 minutes.
4. Stir in the tomato paste, Worcestershire sauce, beef broth, cornstarch, thyme, rosemary, salt, and pepper. Bring the mixture to a boil and then reduce the heat and let it simmer for 5-10 minutes until the sauce has thickened.
5. Transfer the beef mixture to a 9x13-inch baking dish. Spread the mashed potatoes over the top of the beef mixture, using a spatula to create an even layer.
6. Sprinkle the shredded cheddar cheese over the top of the mashed potatoes.
7. Place the baking dish in the Ninja Dual Zone and bake for 20-25 minutes until the cheese is melted and bubbly.
8. Serve hot and enjoy!

Sunday Roast

Serves: 4-6
Prep Time: 10 minutes
Cook Time: 1 hour and 30 minutes
Ninja Dual Zone mode: Roast
Ingredients:
- 1500 g beef roast
- 1 tablespoon olive oil
- 1 teaspoon salt
- 1/2 teaspoon black pepper
- 1 teaspoon garlic powder
- 1 teaspoon dried rosemary
- 1 teaspoon dried thyme
- 1 onion, chopped
- 2 carrots, chopped
- 2 stalks of celery, chopped
- 128g beef broth

Instructions:
1. Preheat the Ninja Dual Zone to 190°C.
2. In a small bowl, mix the salt, black pepper, garlic

powder, rosemary, and thyme.

3. Rub the olive oil all over the beef roast, and then sprinkle the seasoning mixture on all sides of the roast.

4. Place the chopped onion, carrots, and celery in the bottom of the Ninja Dual Zone Ninja Dual .

5. Place the seasoned beef roast on top of the vegetables.

6. Pour the beef broth over the roast.

7. Use the Ninja Dual setting to set the Ninja Dual Zone to Roast, and cook for 1 hour and 30 minutes, or until the internal temperature of the roast reaches 57°C for medium-rare or 62°C for medium.

8. Let the roast rest for 10-15 minutes before slicing and serving with the cooked vegetables and any desired sides.

Steak and Kidney Pie

Serves: 4-6
Prep Time: 20 minutes
Cook Time: 35-40 minutes
Ninja Dual Zone mode: Bake

Ingredients:
- 500 g beef steak, diced
- 226 g beef kidney, diced
- 1 large onion, chopped
- 2 cloves garlic, minced
- 2 tbsp. all-purpose flour
- 104 g of beef broth
- 1 tbsp. Worcestershire sauce
- 1 tbsp. tomato paste
- 1 tbsp. fresh thyme leaves chopped
- 1 tbsp. fresh rosemary leaves chopped
- Salt and pepper to taste
- 1 sheet of puff pastry, thawed
- 1 egg, beaten

Instructions:
1. Preheat the Ninja Dual Zone to 190°C in Bake mode.

2. In a large bowl, combine the diced beef steak and kidney with the chopped onion, minced garlic, and flour. Toss to coat well.

3. In a separate bowl, whisk together the beef broth, Worcestershire sauce, tomato paste, chopped thyme and rosemary, and salt and pepper to taste.

4. Pour the broth mixture over the beef and kidney mixture and stir to combine.

5. Transfer the mixture to a deep baking dish or pie dish.

6. Roll out the puff pastry sheet on a floured surface to fit the top of the dish. Cut a few slits in the top to allow steam to escape.

7. Brush the beaten egg over the top of the puff pastry.

8. Bake in the Ninja Dual Zone for 35-40 minutes, or until the pastry is golden brown and the filling is hot and bubbly.

9. Let cool for a few minutes before serving.

Chicken Korma

Servings: 4-6
Prep Time: 30 minutes
Cook Time: 20 minutes
Ninja Dual Zone mode: Air Fry

Ingredients:
- 750 g boneless, skinless chicken breasts, cut into bite-sized pieces
- 1 onion, chopped
- 4 cloves garlic, minced
- 1-inch piece of ginger, peeled and minced
- 1 tsp ground coriander
- 1 tsp ground cumin
- 1/2 tsp ground turmeric
- 1/4 tsp ground cinnamon
- 1/4 tsp ground cardamom
- 1/4 tsp ground cloves
- 1/4 tsp cayenne pepper
- 1/4 tsp salt
- 32g black pepper
- 64g plain yoghurt
- 32g heavy cream
- 32g chopped fresh cilantro
- 2 tbsp ghee or vegetable oil

Instructions:
1. Preheat the Ninja Dual Zone air fryer to 200°C (200°C).

2. In a mixing bowl, combine the chicken, onion, garlic, ginger, coriander, cumin, turmeric, cinnamon, cardamom, cloves, cayenne pepper, salt, and black pepper. Mix well to ensure the chicken is evenly coated with the spices.

3. Add the chicken mixture to the Ninja Dual air fryer basket and spread it out in a single layer. Select the Air Fry mode and cook for 10 minutes.

4. After 10 minutes, carefully remove the air fryer basket and stir the chicken mixture. Return the basket to the air fryer and continue to cook for

another 5-10 minutes, or until the chicken is cooked through and lightly browned.

5. While the chicken is cooking, in a small saucepan, melt the ghee or vegetable oil over medium heat. Add the yoghurt and cream, and stir to combine. Bring the mixture to a simmer, then reduce the heat to low and simmer for 5 minutes, stirring occasionally.

6. Once the chicken is cooked, remove the air fryer basket from the Ninja Dual Zone and transfer the chicken to a serving dish. Pour the yoghurt and cream sauce over the chicken, and garnish with chopped cilantro.

7. Serve hot with rice or naan.

Roast Chicken with Vegetables

Serves: 4-6
Prep Time: 10 minutes
Cook Time: 1 hour 15 minutes
Ninja Dual Zone mode: Roast

Ingredients:
- 1 whole chicken, about 4-5 pounds
- 4-5 medium potatoes, cut into 1-inch pieces
- 3-4 large carrots, peeled and cut into 1-inch pieces
- 1 onion, cut into wedges
- 2-3 cloves of garlic, minced
- 1 tablespoon olive oil
- 1 teaspoon salt
- 1/2 teaspoon black pepper
- 1 teaspoon paprika
- 1/2 teaspoon dried thyme
- 1/2 teaspoon dried rosemary

Instructions:
1. Preheat the Ninja Dual Zone to Roast mode at 190°C.

2. In a large bowl, combine the potatoes, carrots, onion, garlic, olive oil, salt, pepper, paprika, thyme, and rosemary. Toss to coat the vegetables evenly with the spices and oil.

3. Pat the chicken dry with paper towels, then season the inside and outside of the chicken generously with salt and pepper.

4. Stuff the chicken cavity with some of the vegetable mixtures, reserving the rest for later.

5. Place the chicken on the Ninja Dual Zone's cooking tray or a roasting pan.

6. Arrange the remaining vegetable mixture around the chicken in the cooking tray or roasting pan.

7. Roast the chicken and vegetables in the Ninja

Dual Zone for 1 hour and 15 minutes, or until the chicken is cooked through and the vegetables are tender and caramelized.

8. Let the chicken rest for 10-15 minutes before carving and serving with the roasted vegetables.

Beef and Ale Stew

Serves: 4-6
Prep Time: 20 minutes
Cook Time: 2 hours 15 minutes
Ninja Dual Zone mode: Roast

Ingredients:
- 1000 g beef stew meat, cut into 1-inch cubes
- 2 tbsp all-purpose flour
- - Salt and pepper
- 2 tbsp vegetable oil
- 1 onion, chopped
- 2 cloves garlic, minced
- 3 medium carrots, peeled and chopped
- 2 stalks of celery, chopped
- 256g of beef broth
- 128g ale
- 2 tbsp tomato paste
- 1 tsp dried thyme
- 1 bay leaf
- 128g frozen peas

Instructions:
1. Preheat the Ninja Dual Zone to the "Roast" mode at 190°C.

2. In a large bowl, season the beef with salt and pepper, then toss with flour to coat.

3. Heat the vegetable oil in a Dutch oven over medium-high heat. Add the beef in batches and cook until browned on all sides. Remove the beef and set aside.

4. Add the onion and garlic to the Dutch oven and cook until softened about 5 minutes.

5. Add the carrots and celery and cook for another 5 minutes.

6. Add the beef broth, ale, tomato paste, thyme, and bay leaf. Stir well to combine.

7. Return the beef to the Dutch oven and bring the mixture to a simmer.

8. Cover the Dutch oven with a lid and transfer it to the Ninja Dual Zone Ninja Dual . Cook for 2 hours at 190°C in "Roast" mode, or until the beef is tender.

9. Remove the lid from the Dutch oven and stir in

the frozen peas. Cook for another 5-10 minutes until the peas are heated through.

10. Serve hot with your favourite crusty bread.

Chicken Balti

Serves: 4
Prep Time: 15 minutes
Cook Time: 20 minutes
Ninja Dual Zone mode: Air Fry

Ingredients:

- 4 chicken breasts, cut into bite-sized pieces
- 1 onion, chopped
- 2 garlic cloves, minced
- 1 green chilli pepper, finely chopped
- 1 red bell pepper, chopped
- 2 tbsp balti paste
- 1 tsp garam masala
- 1 tsp ground cumin
- 1 tsp ground coriander
- 1/2 tsp turmeric
- 1/2 tsp paprika
- 64g chicken broth
- 125 ml coconut milk
- Salt and pepper, to taste
- Fresh cilantro, chopped, for garnish

Instructions:

1. Preheat your Ninja Dual Zone to Air Fry mode at 190°C.
2. In a large bowl, mix the balti paste, garam masala, cumin, coriander, turmeric, paprika, salt, and pepper together.
3. Add the chicken pieces to the bowl and mix until the chicken is well-coated.
4. Place the chicken pieces in the Vortex Plus basket and air fry for 8-10 minutes, or until the chicken is cooked through and golden brown.
5. In a separate pan, sauté the onion, garlic, and chilli pepper until the onion is translucent.
6. Add the red bell pepper to the pan and sauté for another 2-3 minutes.
7. Add the chicken broth and coconut milk to the pan and bring to a simmer.
8. Add the chicken to the pan and simmer for an additional 5 minutes, until the sauce has thickened and the chicken is fully coated.
9. Garnish with fresh cilantro and serve hot with rice or naan bread.

Spaghetti Bolognese

Serves: 4-6
Prep Time: 10 minutes
Cook Time: 40 minutes
Ninja Dual Zone mode: Bake

Ingredients:

- 500 g ground beef
- 1 onion, finely chopped
- 3 cloves garlic, minced
- 1 red bell pepper, chopped
- 226 g crushed tomatoes
- 1 teaspoon dried basil
- 1 teaspoon dried oregano
- 1 teaspoon salt
- 1/2 teaspoon black pepper
- 1/4 teaspoon red pepper flakes
- 1 tablespoon olive oil
- 500 g spaghetti
- Grated Parmesan cheese, for serving

Instructions:

1. Preheat the Ninja Dual Zone to sauté mode.
2. Add the olive oil to the inner pot and sauté the onion, garlic and red bell pepper until the onion is translucent about 5 minutes.
3. Add the ground beef to the inner pot and cook, breaking it up with a spatula, until browned about 10 minutes.
4. Add the crushed tomatoes, basil, oregano, salt, black pepper and red pepper flakes to the inner pot and stir to combine.
5. Close the lid and set the Ninja Dual Zone to pressure cook mode on high pressure for 15 minutes.
6. Once the cooking is complete, release the pressure manually and open the lid.
7. Meanwhile, cook the spaghetti according to the package Instructions.
8. Serve the Bolognese sauce over the cooked spaghetti and sprinkle with grated Parmesan cheese. Enjoy!

Thai Green Curry

Serves: 4-6
Prep Time: 15 minutes
Cook Time: 15 minutes
Ninja Dual Zone mode: Air Fry

Ingredients:

- 1 tablespoon vegetable oil

- 2 tablespoons green curry paste
- 500 g of boneless, skinless chicken breasts or thighs, cut into bite-sized pieces
- 400 ml coconut milk
- 128g chicken broth
- 1 red bell pepper, sliced
- 1 green bell pepper, sliced
- 1 onion, sliced
- 2 teaspoons fish sauce
- 1 teaspoon brown sugar
- 1 lime, juiced
- 32g chopped fresh cilantro
- Cooked rice, for serving

Instructions:

1. Set the Ninja Dual Zone to Air Fry mode and preheat to 200°C.
2. Heat the vegetable oil in a large skillet over medium heat. Add the green curry paste and cook for 1-2 minutes until fragrant.
3. Add the chicken to the skillet and cook until browned on all sides, about 5 minutes.
4. Add the coconut milk, chicken broth, bell peppers, onion, fish sauce, and brown sugar to the skillet. Stir to combine.
5. Pour the mixture into the Ninja Dual Zone basket and cook for 10-15 minutes until the chicken is cooked through and the vegetables are tender.
6. Stir in the lime juice and cilantro. Serve over cooked rice.

Beef Bourguignon

Serves 4-6.
Prep Time: 15 minutes
Cook Time: 1 hour and 30 minutes
Ninja Dual Zone mode: Air Fry

Ingredients:

- 1000 g beef chuck, cut into 1-inch pieces
- 2 tbsp all-purpose flour
- Salt and pepper to taste
- 4 tbsp butter
- 1 onion, chopped
- 2 garlic cloves, minced
- 256g of beef broth
- 250 ml of red wine
- 2 tbsp tomato paste
- 2 tsp dried thyme
- 1 bay leaf
- 1 lb baby potatoes, halved

- 128g sliced mushrooms
- 500g frozen pearl onions
- Chopped parsley for garnish

Instructions:

1. Preheat the Ninja Dual Zone to Air Fry mode at 190°C.
2. In a bowl, season the beef with salt and pepper, then coat with flour.
3. In a Dutch oven or oven-safe pot, melt the butter over medium-high heat. Brown the beef in batches, making sure not to overcrowd the pot.
4. Remove the beef and set aside. Add the onion and garlic to the pot and cook until soft and translucent.
5. Add the beef broth, red wine, tomato paste, thyme, and bay leaf to the pot. Stir to combine.
6. Return the beef to the pot and add the potatoes, mushrooms, and pearl onions.
7. Cover the pot with a lid and transfer it to the Ninja Dual Zone Ninja Dual .
8. Cook in Air Fry mode at 190°C for 1 hour and 30 minutes or until the beef is tender.
9. Garnish with chopped parsley before serving.

Sweet and Sour Chicken

Serves: 4
Prep Time: 15 minutes
Cook Time: 15 minutes
Ninja Dual Zone mode: Air Fry

Ingredients:

- 500 g boneless, skinless chicken breasts, cut into bite-sized pieces
- 64g cornstarch
- 1/2 tsp salt
- 1/2 tsp pepper
- 32g vegetable oil
- 1 red bell pepper, diced
- 1 green bell pepper, diced
- 1 onion, diced
- 1 can pineapple chunks, drained
- 64 g ketchup
- 32g white vinegar
- 32g brown sugar
- 1 tbsp soy sauce

Instructions:

1. Preheat the Ninja Dual Zone to Air Fry mode at 200°C.
2. In a bowl, mix the cornstarch, salt, and pepper.
3. Add the chicken to the bowl and toss to coat.

4. Place the coated chicken into the air fryer basket and spray it with cooking oil.
5. Air fry for 10 minutes, flipping the chicken halfway through.
6. In a separate bowl, mix the ketchup, white vinegar, brown sugar, and soy sauce.
7. Heat the vegetable oil in a pan over medium-high heat.
8. Add the bell peppers and onion to the pan and cook until softened.
9. Add the pineapple chunks and the ketchup mixture to the pan and stir.
10. Add the cooked chicken to the pan and stir to coat with the sauce.
11. Serve over rice or with your favourite side dish.

Chicken Katsu Curry

Serves: 4
Prep Time: 15 minutes
Cook Time: 35 minutes
Ninja Dual Zone mode: Air Fry

Ingredients:
- 4 chicken breasts, pounded to an even thickness
- Salt and pepper to taste
- 128g panko breadcrumbs
- 2 eggs, beaten
- 64 g all-purpose flour
- Oil spray
- 1 onion, diced
- 2 garlic cloves, minced
- 1 tablespoon grated ginger
- 2 carrots, peeled and diced
- 2 tablespoons curry powder
- 256g of chicken broth
- 2 tablespoons soy sauce
- 2 tablespoons honey
- 1 tablespoon cornstarch
- Steamed rice, to serve
- Chopped green onions, for garnish

Instructions:
1. Preheat the Ninja Dual Zone to Air Fry mode at 190°C (190°C).
2. Season the chicken breasts with salt and pepper.
3. Place the flour, beaten eggs, and panko breadcrumbs in three separate shallow bowls.
4. Dredge the chicken in flour, shaking off any excess. Dip it in the beaten eggs, then coat it in the panko breadcrumbs.
5. Spray the chicken breasts with oil spray and place them in the Air Fryer basket.
6. Air fry the chicken for 15-20 minutes or until cooked through and crispy.
7. In the meantime, make the curry sauce. Heat a tablespoon of oil in a saucepan over medium heat.
8. Add the onions, garlic, ginger, and carrots. Cook for 5 minutes or until the vegetables are soft.
9. Add the curry powder and stir until fragrant.
10. Pour in the chicken broth, soy sauce, and honey. Bring the mixture to a boil, then reduce the heat and let it simmer for 10-15 minutes.
11. In a small bowl, mix the cornstarch with 1 tablespoon of water to create a slurry. Add it to the curry sauce and stir until thickened.
12. To serve, spoon some rice into each bowl. Top it with a chicken breast and pour some curry sauce over the top. Garnish with chopped green onions. Enjoy!

Lamb Rogan Josh

Serves: 4-6
Prep Time: 20 minutes
Cook Time: 45 minutes
Ninja Dual Zone mode: Bake and Rice Cooker

Ingredients:
- 500 g boneless lamb, cut into cubes
- 1 onion, chopped
- 2 garlic cloves, minced
- 1 tbsp fresh ginger, grated
- 1 tbsp vegetable oil
- 1 tsp cumin seeds
- 1 tsp coriander seeds
- 2 cardamom pods
- 1 cinnamon stick
- 1 bay leaf
- 1 tsp turmeric
- 1 tsp paprika
- 1 tsp garam masala
- 128g canned tomatoes, crushed
- 128g chicken stock
- Salt and pepper to taste
- Chopped fresh cilantro for garnish

For the rice:
- 256g of basmati rice
- 750 ml of water

- Salt to taste

Instructions:

1. In the Ninja Dual Zone Ninja Dual , press the Pressure Cook button and set the timer for 35 minutes. Add the vegetable oil and heat until hot.
2. Add the onion, garlic, and ginger to the Ninja Dual Zone and cook until the onion is translucent, about 3-4 minutes.
3. Add the lamb and cook until browned on all sides, about 5-7 minutes.
4. Add the cumin seeds, coriander seeds, cardamom pods, cinnamon stick, and bay leaf to the Ninja Dual Zone and cook until fragrant, about 1-2 minutes.
5. Add the turmeric, paprika, and garam masala to the Ninja Dual Zone and cook for another minute.
6. Add the crushed tomatoes, chicken stock, salt, and pepper to the Ninja Dual Zone and stir to combine.
7. Close the lid and let the Ninja Dual Zone cook the lamb curry on high pressure for 35 minutes.
8. While the lamb curry is cooking, prepare the rice. In a separate pot, combine the basmati rice, water, and salt. Bring to a boil, then reduce heat to low and simmer for 18 minutes.
9. When the lamb curry is done, release the pressure and open the lid. Serve the lamb curry over the rice and garnish with chopped fresh cilantro. Enjoy!

Pork and Apple Casserole

Serves: 4
Prep Time: 10 minutes
Cook Time: 40 minutes
Ninja Dual Zone mode: Bake

Ingredients:

- 2 tbsp olive oil
- 1 large onion, chopped
- 2 garlic cloves, minced
- 2 pork chops, cubed
- 2 apples, peeled, cored and chopped
- 128g chicken stock
- 1 tbsp honey
- 1 tsp dried thyme
- Salt and pepper to taste
- 256g of mashed potatoes

Instructions:

1. Preheat the Ninja Dual Zone to 190°C.
2. In a large skillet over medium heat, add the olive oil and sauté the onion and garlic for 2-3 minutes, until softened.
3. Add the cubed pork chops to the skillet and cook until browned on all sides, about 5-7 minutes.
4. Add the chopped apples to the skillet and cook for 2-3 minutes, until slightly softened.
5. Pour in the chicken stock, honey, dried thyme, salt, and pepper. Bring to a boil and let simmer for 5 minutes.
6. Pour the pork and apple mixture into a casserole dish. Top with mashed potatoes.
7. Bake in the Ninja Dual Zone for 25-30 minutes, until the mashed potatoes are lightly browned on top.
8. Enjoy while hot.

Vegetable Curry

Serves: 4
Prep Time: 10 minutes
Cook Time: 20-25 minutes
Ninja Dual Zone mode: Air Fry

Ingredients:

- 1 onion, chopped
- 2 cloves garlic, minced
- 1 tbsp ginger, grated
- 2 bell peppers, chopped
- 256g of cauliflower florets
- 128g chopped carrots
- 1 can chickpeas, drained and rinsed
- 1 can diced tomatoes
- 128g vegetable broth
- 1 tbsp curry powder
- 1 tsp ground cumin
- 1 tsp ground coriander
- 1/2 tsp turmeric
- 1/4 tsp cayenne pepper
- Salt and pepper, to taste
- 2 tbsp vegetable oil
- Chopped fresh cilantro, for garnish

Instructions:

1. Preheat your Ninja Dual Zone on Air Fry mode to 190°C.
2. In a large bowl, combine the onion, garlic, ginger, bell peppers, cauliflower, and carrots.
3. Add the chickpeas, diced tomatoes, vegetable

broth, curry powder, cumin, coriander, turmeric, cayenne pepper, salt, and pepper to the bowl. Mix well to combine.

4. Pour the vegetable mixture into the Ninja Dual Zone and drizzle with vegetable oil. Toss to coat.

5. Cook on Air Fry mode for 20-25 minutes, stirring occasionally, until the vegetables are tender and lightly browned.

6. Serve hot with rice and garnish with chopped fresh cilantro.

Mushroom Stroganoff

Serves: 4
Prep Time: 10 minutes
Cook Time: 15 minutes
Ninja Dual Zone mode: Sauté/Crisp Max

Ingredients:
- 1 lb mushrooms, sliced
- 1 onion, chopped
- 3 cloves garlic, minced
- 1 tbsp olive oil
- 1 tbsp butter
- 2 tbsp flour
- 128g vegetable broth
- 1 tbsp tomato paste
- 1 tbsp Dijon mustard
- 1 tbsp Worcestershire sauce
- 64g sour cream
- Salt and pepper to taste
- Chopped fresh parsley, for garnish

Instructions:
1. Preheat the Ninja Dual Zone to Sauté mode and add the olive oil and butter.
2. Add the mushrooms and sauté until they release their moisture and are browned about 5 minutes.
3. Add the onions and garlic and continue to sauté until the onions are translucent about 3 minutes.
4. Stir in the flour and cook for 1 minute.
5. Gradually stir in the vegetable broth, tomato paste, Dijon mustard, and Worcestershire sauce.
6. Switch to Crisp Max mode and cook for 5 minutes, or until the sauce has thickened.
7. Stir in the sour cream and cook for another 2-3 minutes.
8. Season with salt and pepper to taste.
9. Serve hot, garnished with fresh parsley.

Roasted Butternut Squash and Sage Risotto

Serves: 4
Prep Time: 10 minutes
Cook Time: 20 minutes
Ninja Dual Zone mode: Air Fry

Ingredients:
- 1 small butternut squash, peeled and diced
- 1 tbsp olive oil
- Salt and black pepper, to taste
- 1 onion, finely chopped
- 2 cloves garlic, minced
- 128g Arborio rice
- 125 ml of white wine
- 408 g of vegetable broth
- 1 tbsp fresh sage, chopped
- 64g grated Parmesan cheese
- 2 tbsp unsalted butter

Instructions:
1. Preheat the Ninja Dual Zone to 200°C on Air Fry mode.
2. Toss the diced butternut squash with olive oil, salt, and black pepper. Spread it out in a single layer in the Air Fry basket and cook for 10-12 minutes or until tender and lightly browned.
3. In the meantime, heat some olive oil in a saucepan over medium heat. Add the onion and garlic and cook until softened about 5 minutes.
4. Stir in the Arborio rice and cook for 1-2 minutes, stirring constantly.
5. Add the white wine and simmer until it is absorbed into the rice.
6. Slowly add the vegetable broth, about 120g at a time, stirring constantly and waiting for it to be absorbed before adding the next.
7. Once the rice is cooked and the broth is absorbed, stir in the chopped sage, Parmesan cheese, and butter until everything is melted and combined.
8. Finally, fold in the roasted butternut squash and serve hot.

Honey Mustard Glazed Pork Tenderloin

Prep Time: 10 minutes
Marinating time: 1 hour (optional)
Cook Time: 20-25 minutes

Servings: 4
Ninja Dual Zone mode: Air Fry

Ingredients:

1 pork tenderloin, about 1.5 pounds
- 60g Dijon mustard
- 2 tablespoons honey
- 2 tablespoons soy sauce
- 2 cloves garlic, minced
- 1 tablespoon olive oil
- 1/2 teaspoon dried thyme
- Salt and pepper, to taste

Instructions:

1. Preheat the Ninja Dual Zone air fryer to 190°C in Air Fry mode.
2. In a bowl, whisk together the Dijon mustard, honey, soy sauce, minced garlic, olive oil, dried thyme, salt, and pepper to make the glaze.
3. If desired, you can marinate the pork tenderloin in the glaze for enhanced flavour. Place the pork tenderloin in a zip-top bag or a shallow dish, pour the glaze over it, and make sure the tenderloin is coated evenly. Let it marinate in the refrigerator for 1 hour, or up to overnight.
4. Remove the pork tenderloin from the marinade (if marinated) and place it in the lower zone of the Ninja Dual Zone air fryer. Discard any remaining marinade.
5. Close the air fryer and set the timer for 20-25 minutes to cook the pork tenderloin. Adjust the cooking time based on the thickness of the tenderloin and desired level of doneness.
6. After 10-12 minutes, open the air fryer and flip the pork tenderloin using tongs to ensure even cooking. Close the air fryer and continue cooking for the remaining time.
7. Once the pork tenderloin is cooked through and reaches an internal temperature of 63°C for medium doneness, remove it from the air fryer and let it rest for a few minutes before slicing.
8. Slice the pork tenderloin into thin medallions and serve it drizzled with any remaining glaze.

Lemon Herb Roast Chicken

Prep Time: 15 minutes
Cook Time: 40-45 minutes
Servings: 4
Ninja Dual Zone mode: Air Roast

Ingredients:
- 1 whole chicken, about 4 pounds
- 2 lemons
- 4 cloves garlic, minced
- 2 tablespoons fresh thyme leaves
- 2 tablespoons fresh rosemary leaves
- 2 tablespoons olive oil
- Salt and pepper, to taste

Instructions:

1. Preheat the Ninja Dual Zone air fryer to 190°C in Air Roast mode.
2. Rinse the whole chicken under cold water and pat it dry with paper towels.
3. Cut one lemon into slices. Set aside.
4. In a small bowl, combine the minced garlic, fresh thyme leaves, fresh rosemary leaves, olive oil, salt, and pepper to make a herb mixture.
5. Carefully loosen the skin of the chicken by gently sliding your fingers between the skin and the meat, being careful not to tear the skin.
6. Rub the herb mixture evenly over the chicken, including underneath the skin. Make sure to coat the chicken thoroughly with the mixture.
7. Place the lemon slices inside the cavity of the chicken.
8. Open the air fryer and place the seasoned and stuffed chicken in the lower zone of the Ninja Dual Zone air fryer. Close the air fryer and set the timer for 40-45 minutes to roast the chicken.
9. After 20-25 minutes, open the air fryer and carefully flip the chicken using tongs for even browning. Close the air fryer and continue cooking for the remaining time, or until the chicken reaches an internal temperature of 74°C and the skin is golden brown and crispy.
10. Once the chicken is cooked through, remove it from the air fryer and let it rest for a few minutes before carving.
11. Squeeze the juice of the remaining lemon over the roasted chicken for added flavour.

Pesto Chicken Pasta

Prep Time: 15 minutes
Cook Time: 20 minutes
Servings: 4
Ninja Dual Zone mode: Air Fry

Ingredients:
- 230g pasta(such as penne or fusilli)

- 2 boneless, skinless chicken breasts
- Salt and pepper, to taste
- 1 tablespoon olive oil
- 120g basil pesto
- 150g cherry tomatoes, halved
- 50g grated Parmesan cheese
- Fresh basil leaves, for garnish

Instructions:

1. Preheat the Ninja Dual Zone air fryer to 190°C in Air Fry mode.
2. Cook the pasta according to the package instructions until al dente. Drain and set aside.
3. While the pasta is cooking, season the chicken breasts with salt and pepper on both sides.
4. Open the air fryer and place the seasoned chicken breasts in the lower zone. Close the air fryer and set the timer for 12-15 minutes to cook the chicken.
5. After 6-7 minutes, open the air fryer and flip the chicken breasts using tongs to ensure even cooking. Close the air fryer and continue cooking for the remaining time, or until the chicken is cooked through and reaches an internal temperature of 74°C.
6. Remove the chicken from the air fryer and let it rest for a few minutes. Slice the chicken into thin strips.
7. In a large bowl, combine the cooked pasta, basil pesto, cherry tomatoes, and grated Parmesan cheese. Toss until the pasta is evenly coated with the pesto sauce.
8. Open the air fryer and place the pasta mixture in the lower zone. Close the air fryer and set the timer for 3-5 minutes to warm the pasta and slightly melt the cheese.
9. Once the pasta is warmed through, remove it from the air fryer and transfer it to serving plates or a serving dish.
10. Top the pasta with the sliced chicken and garnish with fresh basil leaves.

Baked Cod with Herbed Breadcrumbs

Prep Time: 15 minutes
Cook Time: 12 minutes
Servings: 4
Ninja Dual Zone mode: Air Fry

Ingredients:
- 4 cod fillets (about 150g each)
- 55g panko breadcrumbs
- 2 tablespoons grated Parmesan cheese
- 1 tablespoon fresh parsley, chopped
- 1 tablespoon fresh dill, chopped
- 1 teaspoon lemon zest
- 2 tablespoons melted butter
- Salt and pepper, to taste
- Lemon wedges, for serving

Instructions:

1. Preheat the Ninja Dual Zone air fryer to 200°C in Air Fry mode.
2. In a bowl, combine the panko breadcrumbs, grated Parmesan cheese, chopped parsley, chopped dill, lemon zest, melted butter, salt, and pepper. Mix well to create the herbed breadcrumb mixture.
3. Pat dry the cod fillets with a paper towel to remove any excess moisture.
4. Dip each cod fillet into the herbed breadcrumb mixture, pressing gently to adhere the breadcrumbs to the fish.
5. Place the breaded cod fillets in Zone 1 of the Ninja Dual Zone. Air fry for about 10-12 minutes, or until the fish is cooked through and the breadcrumbs are golden brown and crispy.
6. Carefully remove the baked cod fillets from the air fryer.
7. Serve the Baked Cod with Herbed Breadcrumbs hot, accompanied by lemon wedges for squeezing over the fish.
8. This dish pairs well with a side of roasted vegetables or a fresh salad.

Honey Glazed Gammon

Prep Time: 10 minutes
Cook Time: 1 hour 30 minutes
Servings: 4-6
Ninja Dual Zone mode: Air Roast

Ingredients:
1500g (3.3 lbs) gammon joint (uncured, boneless)
- 120ml honey
- 2 tablespoons Dijon mustard
- 2 tablespoons apple cider vinegar
- 1 teaspoon ground cinnamon
- 1/2 teaspoon ground cloves
- 1/2 teaspoon ground nutmeg

- Salt and pepper, to taste

Instructions:

1. Preheat the Ninja Dual Zone air fryer to 190°C in Air Roast mode.
2. In a small bowl, whisk together the honey, Dijon mustard, apple cider vinegar, ground cinnamon, ground cloves, ground nutmeg, salt, and pepper to make the glaze.
3. Place the gammon joint in the lower zone of the Ninja Dual Zone air fryer. Close the air fryer and set the timer for 1 hour.
4. After 1 hour, open the air fryer and carefully remove the gammon joint. Using a sharp knife, score the surface of the gammon by making diagonal cuts about 1 inch apart in a crisscross pattern.
5. Brush the glaze generously over the scored gammon joint, making sure to coat all sides.
6. Place the glazed gammon joint back in the lower zone of the air fryer. Close the air fryer and set the timer for an additional 30 minutes.
7. After 15 minutes, open the air fryer and brush the gammon joint with more glaze. Close the air fryer and continue cooking for the remaining time.
8. Once the gammon is cooked through and reaches an internal temperature of 71°C, remove it from the air fryer and let it rest for a few minutes before slicing.
9. Slice the Honey Glazed Gammon into desired thickness and serve it with your favourite sides such as roasted potatoes, steamed vegetables, or a fresh salad.

Lamb Chops with Mint Sauce

Prep Time: 10 minutes
Cook Time: 12-15 minutes
Servings: 4
Ninja Dual Zone mode: Air Roast

Ingredients:
- 8 lamb chops
- Salt and pepper, to taste
- 2 tablespoons olive oil
- 4g fresh mint leaves, finely chopped
- 2 tablespoons lemon juice
- 2 tablespoons honey
- 1 tablespoon Dijon mustard

- 1 tablespoon apple cider vinegar

Instructions:

1. Preheat the Ninja Dual Zone air fryer to 190°C in Air Roast mode.
2. Season the lamb chops with salt and pepper on both sides.
3. Open the air fryer and place the seasoned lamb chops in the lower zone. Close the air fryer and set the timer for 12-15 minutes to cook the lamb chops.
4. After 6-7 minutes, open the air fryer and flip the lamb chops using tongs for even cooking. Close the air fryer and continue cooking for the remaining time, or until the lamb chops reach your desired level of doneness.
5. While the lamb chops are cooking, prepare the mint sauce. In a small bowl, combine the finely chopped mint leaves, lemon juice, honey, Dijon mustard, and apple cider vinegar. Stir well to combine.
6. Once the lamb chops are cooked to your liking, remove them from the air fryer and let them rest for a few minutes.
7. Serve the lamb chops with the mint sauce on the side or drizzled over the top.

Stuffed Bell Peppers

Prep Time: 20 minutes
Cook Time: 25-30 minutes
Servings: 4
Ninja Dual Zone mode: Air Roast

Ingredients:
- 4 large bell peppers (any colour)
- 1 pound ground beef (or ground turkey)
- 1 small onion, diced
- 2 cloves garlic, minced
- 200g cooked rice
- 240g tomato sauce
- 1 teaspoon dried oregano
- 1 teaspoon dried basil
- ½ teaspoon paprika
- Salt and pepper, to taste
- 110 shredded mozzarella cheese
- Fresh parsley, for garnish

Instructions:

1. Preheat the Ninja Dual Zone air fryer to 190°C in Air Roast mode.

2. Cut off the tops of the bell peppers and remove the seeds and membranes. Set aside.

3. In a skillet, brown the ground beef over medium heat until cooked through. Drain any excess fat.

4. Add the diced onion and minced garlic to the skillet with the ground beef. Cook until the onion is softened and translucent.

5. Stir in the cooked rice, tomato sauce, dried oregano, dried basil, paprika, salt, and pepper. Cook for a few more minutes to allow the flavours to meld together.

6. Stuff the mixture into the hollowed-out bell peppers, pressing it down gently. Fill each pepper until it's full and slightly overflowing.

7. Open the air fryer and place the stuffed bell peppers in the lower zone. Close the air fryer and set the timer for 25-30 minutes to cook the peppers.

8. After 15-20 minutes, open the air fryer and sprinkle the shredded mozzarella cheese evenly over the stuffed bell peppers. Close the air fryer and continue cooking for the remaining time, or until the cheese is melted and bubbly.

9. Once the stuffed bell peppers are cooked and the cheese is melted, remove them from the air fryer and let them cool for a few minutes.

10. Garnish with fresh parsley before serving.

Teriyaki Salmon

Prep Time: 10 minutes
Marinating time: 30 minutes
Cook Time: 12-15 minutes
Servings: 4
Ninja Dual Zone mode: Air Roast

Ingredients:

- 4 salmon fillets
- 55g soy sauce
- 2 tablespoons honey
- 2 tablespoons rice vinegar
- 1 tablespoon sesame oil
- 2 cloves garlic, minced
- 1 teaspoon grated ginger
- 1 tablespoon cornstarch
- 2 tablespoons water
- Sesame seeds, for garnish
- Sliced green onions, for garnish

Instructions:

1. Preheat the Ninja Dual Zone air fryer to 190°C in Air Roast mode.

2. In a small bowl, whisk together the soy sauce, honey, rice vinegar, sesame oil, minced garlic, and grated ginger to make the teriyaki sauce.

3. Place the salmon fillets in a shallow dish or a zip-top bag. Pour half of the teriyaki sauce over the salmon, reserving the remaining sauce for later. Make sure the salmon is evenly coated in the sauce. Marinate the salmon in the refrigerator for at least 30 minutes.

4. In a separate small bowl, mix the cornstarch and water to create a slurry.

5. Open the air fryer and place the marinated salmon fillets in the lower zone. Close the air fryer and set the timer for 12-15 minutes to cook the salmon.

6. While the salmon is cooking, pour the reserved teriyaki sauce into a small saucepan. Add the cornstarch slurry and heat over medium heat. Stir continuously until the sauce thickens and becomes glossy. Remove from heat.

7. After 6-7 minutes, open the air fryer and brush some of the thickened teriyaki sauce over the salmon fillets. Close the air fryer and continue cooking for the remaining time.

8. Once the salmon is cooked through and flakes easily with a fork, remove it from the air fryer.

9. Serve the Teriyaki Salmon fillets drizzled with the remaining thickened teriyaki sauce. Sprinkle sesame seeds and sliced green onions on top for garnish.

Sea Bass with Balsamic Tomatoes

Prep Time: 10 minutes
Cook Time: 20 minutes
Servings: 4
Ninja Dual Zone mode: Air Fry

Ingredients

- 4 (160g each) sea bass fillets
- 1 medium lemon, zest and juice
- Sea salt and ground black pepper, to taste
- 1 tsp red pepper flakes, crushed
- 1 tsp garlic granules
- 500g cherry tomatoes
- 60ml balsamic vinegar
- 1 tbsp olive oil

Instructions:

1. Insert a crisper plate into the zone 1 drawer.

Spray the crisper plate with nonstick cooking oil.

2. Pat the fish dry with tea towels. Toss the fish fillets with lemon, salt, black pepper, red pepper, and garlic granules. Spray them with nonstick cooking oil.

3. Toss the cherry tomatoes with balsamic vinegar, olive oil, salt, and black pepper.

4. Place the sea bass fillets in the zone 1 drawer. Place the cherry tomatoes in the zone 2 drawer (with no crisper plate inserted).

5. Select zone 1 and pair it with "AIR FRY" at 190°C for 20 minutes. Select zone 2 and pair it with "ROAST" at 200°C for 15 minutes. Select "SYNC" followed by the "START/STOP" button.

Dijon Herb Meatloaf

Prep Time: 10 minutes
Cook Time: 20 minutes
Servings: 6
Ninja Dual Zone mode: Air Fry

Ingredients

- 300g pork mince
- 300g beef mince
- 1 medium egg, well-beaten
- 1 medium onion, chopped
- 2 garlic cloves, minced
- 1 tbsp dried rosemary leaves, crushed
- 1 tbsp dried thyme leaves, crushed
- 60g tortilla chips, crushed
- 1 tbsp olive oil
- 170ml tomato paste
- 1 tbsp Dijon mustard

Instructions:

1. Brush 2 loaf tins with nonstick cooking oil.

2. In a mixing bowl, thoroughly combine the pork mince, beef mince, egg, onion, garlic, rosemary, thyme, and tortilla chips. Brush the meatloaves with olive oil.

3. Mix the tomato paste with Dijon mustard and reserve.

4. Press the meat mixture into the loaf tins. Add a loaf tin to each drawer.

5. Select zone 1 and pair it with "AIR FRY" at 180°C for 20 minutes. Select "MATCH" to duplicate settings across both zones. Press the "START/STOP" button.

6. When zone 1 time reaches 10 minutes, spread the tomato mixture over the meatloaves and bake for a further 10 minutes, until the centre of your meatloaf reaches 74°C. Reinsert the drawer to continue cooking.

Mini Meatloaves

Prep Time: 10 minutes
Cook Time: 20 minutes
Servings: 4
Ninja Dual Zone mode: Air Fry

Ingredients

- 200g beef mince
- 300g pork mince
- 1 egg, well-beaten
- 1 tbsp olive oil
- 1 medium onion, chopped
- 2 garlic cloves, minced
- 1 small bell pepper, seeded and chopped
- 60g fresh breadcrumbs
- 170ml tomato paste
- 1 tsp molasses

Instructions:

1. Brush 4 large ramekins with nonstick cooking oil.

2. Mix the beef mince, pork mince, egg, olive oil, onion, garlic, bell pepper, and breadcrumbs.

3. Mix the tomato paste with molasses and reserve.

4. Press the mince mixture into the prepared ramekins. Place the ramekins in both drawers.

5. Select zone 1 and pair it with "AIR FRY" at 180°C for 20 minutes. Select "MATCH" to duplicate settings across both zones. Press the "START/STOP" button.

6. When zone 1 time reaches 10 minutes, spread the tomato mixture over the meatloaves and bake for a further 10 minutes, until the centre of your meatloaf reaches 74°C. Reinsert the drawers to continue cooking.

Restaurant-Style Burgers

Prep Time: 5 minutes
Cook Time: 15 minutes
Servings: 3
Ninja Dual Zone mode: Air Fry

Ingredients

- 300g lean beef mince
- 300g pork mince

- 1 medium onion, chopped
- 2 garlic cloves, minced
- 30g seasoned breadcrumbs
- Sea salt and ground black pepper, to taste
- 1/2 tsp red pepper flakes, crushed
- 4 burger buns
- 1 medium tomato, sliced
- 8 Romaine lettuce
- 1 small onion, thinly sliced

Instructions:

1. Insert a crisper plate in each drawer. Spray the crisper plates with nonstick cooking oil.
2. Thoroughly combine the beef mince, pork mince, 1 medium onion, garlic, breadcrumbs, and spices. Shape the mixture into four patties and spray them with cooking oil.
3. Add burgers to each drawer.
4. Select zone 1 and pair it with "AIR FRY" at 190°C for 15 minutes. Select "MATCH" to duplicate settings across both zones. Press the "START/STOP" button.
5. When zone 1 time reaches 7 minutes, turn the burgers over and spray them with cooking oil on the other side. Reinsert the drawer to continue cooking.
6. Serve your burgers in the buns topped with tomato, lettuce, and onion.

Buckwheat & Garbanzo Bean Burgers

Prep Time: 10 minutes
Cook Time: 20 minutes
Servings: 6
Ninja Dual Zone mode: Air Fry

Ingredients

- 1 (400g) can garbanzo beans, rinsed and drained
- 200g buckwheat, soaked overnight, drained and rinsed
- 1 large onion, chopped
- 2 medium garlic cloves, minced
- 100g breadcrumbs
- Sea salt and ground black pepper, to taste
- 1 tsp smoked paprika
- 1/2 tsp cumin seeds
- 150ml BBQ sauce

Instructions:

1. Insert the crisper plates in both drawers and spray them with cooking oil.

2. In your blender or a food processor, thoroughly combine all the Ingredients. Shape the mixture into 6 patties and spray them with nonstick cooking oil. Now, arrange them in the lightly-greased drawers.
3. Select zone 1 and pair it with "AIR FRY" at 190°C for 20 minutes. Select "MATCH" to duplicate settings across both zones. Press the "START/STOP" button.
4. When zone 1 time reaches 10 minutes, turn the burgers over, spray them with cooking oil on the other side, and reinsert the drawers to continue cooking.
5. Serve burger patties in hamburger buns with toppings of choice.

Holiday Roast

Prep Time: 10 minutes
Cook Time: 1 hour
Servings:4
Ninja Dual Zone mode: Air Fry

Ingredients

- 800g Boston butt, cut into 4 pieces
- Marinade:
- 100ml dry red wine
- 1 tbsp Dijon mustard
- 1 tbsp hot paprika
- 50ml tomato sauce
- Sea salt and ground black pepper
- 2 tbsp olive oil

Instructions:

1. Mix all the marinade Ingredients. Add Boston butt to the marinade and let it sit for about 1 hour in your fridge.
2. Insert crisper plates in both drawers. Spray the crisper plates with nonstick cooking oil.
3. Remove the Boston butt from the marinade. Place the Boston butt in both drawers. Select zone 1 and pair it with "AIR FRY" at 175°C for 55 minutes to 1 hour. Select "MATCH" to duplicate settings across both zones. Press the "START/STOP" button.
4. At the halfway point, turn the Boston butt over, brush them with the reserved marinade and reinsert the drawers to resume cooking.

Chapter 4: British Classics

Fish Pie

Serves: 4-6
Prep Time: 30 minutes
Cook Time: 30 minutes
Ninja Dual Zone mode: Bake

Ingredients:

- 500g white fish (such as cod or haddock), skinned and cut into chunks
- 200g raw prawns, shelled
- 600g potatoes, peeled and chopped
- 150ml whole milk
- 50g butter
- 50g plain flour
- 1 onion, chopped
- 2 garlic cloves, minced
- 1 carrot, chopped
- 100g frozen peas
- 100g frozen sweetcorn
- 500ml fish stock
- 1 tbsp chopped fresh parsley
- 1 tbsp chopped fresh thyme
- Salt and pepper to taste

Instructions:

1. Preheat the Ninja Dual Zone to Bake mode at 200°C.
2. In a large saucepan, boil the chopped potatoes until soft. Drain and mash them with the milk and half of the butter. Season with salt and pepper and set aside.
3. In a large frying pan, melt the remaining butter over medium heat. Add the onion, garlic, and carrot and sauté for 5 minutes or until the vegetables are softened.
4. Add the plain flour to the pan and cook for a further 2 minutes.
5. Gradually add the fish stock to the pan, stirring constantly to prevent any lumps from forming. Simmer for 5 minutes until the sauce has thickened.
6. Add the white fish, prawns, frozen peas, sweetcorn, chopped parsley, and thyme to the saucepan. Stir well to combine.
7. Transfer the fish and vegetable mixture to an ovenproof dish and top with the mashed potato mixture.
8. Bake in the Ninja Dual Zone for 30 minutes or until the top is golden brown and the filling is bubbling.
9. Serve hot with steamed vegetables or a side salad. Enjoy!

Cullen Skink (smoked haddock soup)

Serves 4-6
Prep Time: 10 minutes
Cook Time: 40 minutes
Ninja Dual Zone mode: Bake

Ingredients:

- 500g smoked haddock fillet
- 1 onion, chopped
- 2 large potatoes, peeled and chopped
- 500ml chicken or fish stock
- 200ml whole milk
- 100ml double cream
- 2 tbsp unsalted butter
- Salt and pepper, to taste

Instructions:

1. Preheat the Ninja Dual Zone to the Bake mode at 190°C.
2. Place the smoked haddock fillet in a baking dish and bake for 10-15 minutes until cooked through.
3. Once cooked, remove the haddock from the baking dish and set aside to cool.
4. In a large saucepan, melt the butter over medium heat. Add the chopped onion and cook until softened about 5 minutes.
5. Add the chopped potatoes to the saucepan, and pour in the chicken or fish stock. Bring to a boil, then reduce the heat and simmer for 15-20 minutes or until the potatoes are soft and cooked through.
6. Remove the skin and bones from the cooled smoked haddock fillet and flake the flesh into chunks.
7. Add the smoked haddock to the saucepan with the potato and stock mixture, and stir in the whole milk and double cream.
8. Bring the soup to a gentle simmer, and cook for a further 5-10 minutes until heated through. Season with salt and pepper to taste.
9. Serve hot, garnished with chopped parsley or chives if desired.

Vegetarian Chili

Serves: 6-8
Prep Time: 15 minutes
Cook Time: 3-4 hours on High or 6-8 hours on Low in Slow Cook mode
Ninja Dual Zone mode: Sauté mode to sauté vegetables and Slow Cook mode to cook the chilli.

Ingredients:

- 2 tablespoons olive oil
- 1 onion, chopped
- 3 cloves garlic, minced
- 1 red bell pepper, chopped
- 1 green bell pepper, chopped
- 2 carrots, peeled and chopped
- 2 stalks of celery, chopped
- 2 tablespoons chilli powder
- 1 tablespoon ground cumin
- 1 teaspoon smoked paprika
- 1 teaspoon dried oregano
- 1/2 teaspoon salt
- 1/4 teaspoon black pepper
- 2 cans of black beans, drained and rinsed
- 2 cans of diced tomatoes
- 1 can of tomato paste
- 128g vegetable broth
- 128g frozen corn kernels

Instructions:

1. Set the Ninja Dual Zone to Sauté mode and add the olive oil. Once the oil is hot, add the onion and garlic and cook until softened about 3-4 minutes.
2. Add the bell peppers, carrots, and celery and cook for an additional 5 minutes, stirring occasionally.
3. Stir in the chilli powder, cumin, smoked paprika, oregano, salt, and black pepper, and cook for 1-2 minutes until fragrant.
4. Add the black beans, diced tomatoes, tomato paste, and vegetable broth. Stir to combine and bring the mixture to a simmer.
5. Cancel the Sauté mode and switch the Ninja Dual Zone to Slow Cook mode. Cover and cook on High for 3-4 hours or on Low for 6-8 hours.
6. Stir in the frozen corn kernels during the last 30 minutes of cooking.
7. Serve the vegetarian chilli hot, topped with your choice of garnishes, such as shredded cheese, sour cream, diced avocado, or chopped fresh cilantro.

Ratatouille

Serves: 4
Prep Time: 15 minutes
Cook Time: 20-25 minutes
Ninja Dual Zone mode: Air Fry

Ingredients:

- 1 large eggplant, cut into 1-inch cubes
- 2 zucchinis, cut into 1-inch cubes
- 1 large onion, chopped
- 4 cloves garlic, minced
- 1 red bell pepper, chopped
- 1 yellow bell pepper, chopped
- 1 can diced tomatoes
- 1 tsp dried thyme
- 1 tsp dried oregano
- Salt and black pepper, to taste
- 60 ml olive oil

Instructions:

1. Preheat the Ninja Dual Zone to Air Fry mode at 190°C.
2. In a large bowl, combine the eggplant, zucchini, onion, garlic, red bell pepper, yellow bell pepper, thyme, oregano, salt, black pepper, and olive oil. Mix well to coat the vegetables evenly.
3. Place the seasoned vegetables in the Ninja Dual basket and air fry for 15 minutes, stirring occasionally.
4. Add the can of diced tomatoes to the basket and stir well to combine.
5. Air fry for another 5-10 minutes, until the vegetables are tender and the tomatoes are heated through.
6. Serve the ratatouille hot as a side dish or over rice or quinoa for a complete meal.

Chicken and Mushroom Pie

Serves: 4-6
Prep Time: 20 minutes
Cook Time: 30 minutes
Ninja Dual Zone mode: Bake

Ingredients:

- 450g chicken breast, diced
- 220g mushrooms, sliced
- 1 onion, diced
- 2 garlic cloves, minced
- 2 tbsp olive oil
- 2 tbsp butter
- 2 tbsp all-purpose flour
- 120g chicken stock

- 60g heavy cream
- 1 tsp dried thyme
- Salt and pepper
- 1 sheet of puff pastry, thawed
- 1 egg, beaten

Instructions:

1. Preheat the Ninja Dual Zone to 190°C using the Ninja Dual mode.
2. In a large skillet, heat the olive oil over medium-high heat. Add the chicken and cook until browned on all sides. Remove from the skillet and set aside.
3. In the same skillet, melt the butter over medium heat. Add the onions and garlic and cook until softened.
4. Add the sliced mushrooms to the skillet and cook until browned.
5. Sprinkle the flour over the mushrooms and onions and stir until coated.
6. Gradually add the chicken stock to the skillet, stirring constantly.
7. Add the heavy cream and dried thyme to the skillet and stir to combine. Season with salt and pepper to taste.
8. Return the chicken to the skillet and stir to combine.
9. Transfer the chicken and mushroom mixture to a baking dish.
10. Roll out the puff pastry sheet and place it over the top of the baking dish. Use a sharp knife to cut a few slits in the pastry to allow steam to escape.
11. Brush the beaten egg over the top of the pastry.
12. Place the baking dish into the Ninja Dual Zone using the Ninja Dual mode and bake for 25-30 minutes or until the pastry is golden brown and puffed up.
13. Serve hot and enjoy!

Cumberland Sausage and Mash

Serves: 4
Prep Time: 10 minutes
Cook Time: 15-20 minutes
Ninja Dual Zone mode: Air Fry

Ingredients:

- 4 Cumberland sausages
- 4 large potatoes, peeled and cubed
- 1 onion, chopped
- 2 cloves garlic, minced
- 2 tbsp butter
- 30g milk

- Salt and pepper to taste
- Gravy (optional)

Instructions:

1. Preheat your Ninja Dual Zone to Air Fry mode at 190°C (190°C).
2. Place the sausages in the air fryer basket and cook for 10-12 minutes or until golden brown, turning halfway through.
3. Meanwhile, boil the potatoes in a pot of salted water until soft.
4. In a separate pan, sauté the onion and garlic in the butter until soft.
5. Drain the potatoes and add the sautéed onion and garlic. Mash the potatoes with a potato masher or fork, adding the milk gradually to reach your desired consistency. Season with salt and pepper to taste.
6. Serve the sausages on top of the mashed potatoes, and pour gravy over the top if desired. Enjoy!

Steak and Ale Pie

Serves: 4-6
Prep Time: 20 minutes
Cook Time: 1 hour and 30 minutes
Ninja Dual Zone mode: Bake

Ingredients:

- 1000g of beef stew meat, cut into small cubes
- 1 onion, chopped
- 2 cloves of garlic, minced
- 250g of beef stock
- 120g of ale
- 2 tablespoons of tomato paste
- 2 teaspoons of Worcestershire sauce
- 1 teaspoon of dried thyme
- 1 teaspoon of dried rosemary
- Salt and pepper to taste
- 1 sheet of puff pastry, thawed
- 1 egg, beaten

Instructions:

1. Preheat the Ninja Dual Zone to the Bake mode at 190°C.
2. In a large pot or Dutch oven, brown the beef stew meat over medium-high heat. Remove the beef from the pot and set aside.
3. In the same pot, add the onion and garlic and cook until softened.
4. Add the beef stock, ale, tomato paste, Worcestershire sauce, thyme, and rosemary to the pot. Stir well.
5. Add the browned beef back into the pot and bring

the mixture to a boil.

6. Reduce the heat to low and let the mixture simmer for 1 hour, or until the beef is tender.

7. Transfer the beef mixture to a pie dish.

8. Roll out the puff pastry and place it on top of the beef mixture, tucking in the edges.

9. Brush the beaten egg over the puff pastry.

10. Place the pie dish in the Ninja Dual Zone and cook in the Bake mode at 190°C for 25-30 minutes, or until the pastry is golden brown and puffed up.

11. Serve hot and enjoy!

Ploughman's Salad

Serves: 4
Prep Time: 15 minutes
Cook Time: 10 minutes
Ninja Dual Zone mode: Air Fry

Ingredients:

- 1 head of lettuce, washed and chopped
- 1/2 red onion, thinly sliced
- 2 tomatoes, chopped
- 1/2 cucumber, sliced
- 30g of pickles, sliced
- 32g of cheddar cheese, cubed
- 30g of cooked ham, cubed
- 30g of salad dressing (such as ranch or vinaigrette)

Instructions:

1. Preheat your Ninja Dual Zone to 200°C on Air Fry mode.

2. Place the ham cubes in the Air Fryer basket and cook for 5 minutes until crispy. Remove and set aside.

3. In a large mixing bowl, combine the lettuce, red onion, tomatoes, cucumber, pickles, and cheddar cheese. Toss well.

4. Add the crispy ham to the salad mixture and toss again.

5. Drizzle the salad dressing over the top and toss until everything is coated evenly.

6. Serve the salad immediately and enjoy!

Salmon en Croute

Serves: 4-6
Prep Time: 30 minutes
Cook Time: 20-25 minutes
Ninja Dual Zone mode: Bake

Ingredients:

- 1 sheet puff pastry, thawed
- 450g fresh salmon fillet, skin removed
- Salt and pepper, to taste
- 1 egg, beaten
- 60g cream cheese, softened
- 2 tbsp (30 ml) chopped fresh dill
- 2 tbsp (30 ml) chopped fresh parsley
- 1 garlic clove, minced
- Juice of 1/2 lemon
- 30g breadcrumbs
- 32g grated Parmesan cheese

Instructions:

1. Preheat the Ninja Dual Zone to Bake at 190°C (190°C).

2. Season the salmon fillet with salt and pepper, and set aside.

3. In a mixing bowl, combine the cream cheese, dill, parsley, garlic, and lemon juice, and mix until smooth.

4. On a lightly floured surface, roll out the puff pastry sheet to a thickness of about 1/4 inch (6 mm).

5. Place the salmon fillet in the centre of the pastry sheet.

6. Spread the cream cheese mixture over the top of the salmon fillet.

7. In a separate bowl, mix the breadcrumbs and Parmesan cheese, and sprinkle the mixture over the cream cheese mixture.

8. Fold the pastry over the salmon, tucking in the edges to seal it.

9. Place the pastry-wrapped salmon seam-side down onto a baking tray lined with parchment paper.

10. Brush the beaten egg over the top of the pastry.

11. Using a sharp knife, make a few small slits on the top of the pastry to allow steam to escape.

12. Place the baking tray into the Ninja Dual Zone and bake for 20-25 minutes, or until the pastry is golden brown and the salmon is cooked through.

13. Remove the baking tray from the Ninja Dual Zone and let the Salmon en Croute rest for a few minutes before slicing and serving.

Vegetable Lasagna

Serves: 6-8
Prep Time: 20 minutes
Cook Time: 40-45 minutes
Ninja Dual Zone mode: Bake

Ingredients:

- 9 lasagna noodles
- 1 tbsp olive oil
- 1 medium onion, diced
- 2 cloves garlic, minced
- 1 medium zucchini, sliced

- 1 red bell pepper, diced
- 1 yellow squash, sliced
- 226g sliced mushrooms
- 1/2 tsp dried oregano
- 1/2 tsp dried basil
- Salt and pepper to taste
- 1 jar (24 oz) pasta sauce
- 128g ricotta cheese
- 250g of shredded mozzarella cheese
- 64g grated Parmesan cheese

Instructions:

1. Preheat the Ninja Dual Zone to 190°C using the Bake mode.
2. Cook the lasagna noodles according to package directions. Drain and set aside.
3. Heat the olive oil in a large skillet over medium heat. Add the onion and garlic and cook until soft and fragrant, about 3-4 minutes.
4. Add the zucchini, red bell pepper, yellow squash, mushrooms, oregano, basil, salt, and pepper. Cook until the vegetables are tender, about 8-10 minutes.
5. Spread a thin layer of pasta sauce on the bottom of a 9x13-inch baking dish.
6. Arrange 3 cooked lasagna noodles in a single layer over the sauce.
7. Spread half of the ricotta cheese over the noodles.
8. Spread half of the vegetable mixture over the ricotta.
9. Spread 120g of pasta sauce over the vegetables.
10. Sprinkle 120g of shredded mozzarella cheese over the sauce.
11. Repeat layers of lasagna noodles, ricotta cheese, vegetables, pasta sauce, and mozzarella cheese.
12. Top with a layer of grated Parmesan cheese.
13. Cover the baking dish with foil and bake for 25 minutes.
14. Remove the foil and bake for an additional 10-15 minutes, or until the cheese is melted and bubbly.
15. Let the lasagna cool for a few minutes before slicing and serving.

Chicken Tikka Pie

Prep Time: 20 minutes
Cook Time: 30-35 minutes
Servings: 4
Ninja Dual Zone mode: Air Roast

Ingredients:
For the filling:
- 2 boneless, skinless chicken breasts, cut into bite-sized pieces
- 250ml plain yoghourt
- 2 tablespoons tikka masala paste
- 1 tablespoon lemon juice
- 1 teaspoon ground cumin
- 1 teaspoon ground coriander
- 1/2 teaspoon ground turmeric
- 1/2 teaspoon paprika
- 1/2 teaspoon salt
- 1/4 teaspoon black pepper
- 2 tablespoons vegetable oil
- 1 onion, finely chopped
- 2 cloves garlic, minced
- 1-inch piece ginger, grated
- 1 red bell pepper, diced
- 70 frozen peas
- 5g chopped fresh cilantro (coriander)
- Salt and pepper, to taste

For the pastry:
- 1 sheet puff pastry, thawed
- 1 egg, beaten (for egg wash)

Instructions:

1. Preheat the Ninja Dual Zone air fryer to 190°C in Air Roast mode.
2. In a bowl, combine the yogurt, tikka masala paste, lemon juice, ground cumin, ground coriander, ground turmeric, paprika, salt, and black pepper. Add the chicken pieces to the marinade and toss to coat. Let it marinate for at least 15 minutes, or up to overnight in the refrigerator.
3. In a large skillet, heat the vegetable oil over medium heat. Add the chopped onion and cook until softened and translucent. Add the minced garlic and grated ginger, and cook for an additional minute.
4. Add the marinated chicken to the skillet (reserving the marinade), and cook until the chicken is browned and cooked through. Stir in the diced bell pepper and frozen peas, and cook for a few more minutes until the vegetables are tender.
5. Pour the reserved marinade into the skillet, stirring well to combine. Cook for another 2-3 minutes until the sauce thickens slightly. Remove from heat and stir in the chopped fresh cilantro. Season with salt and pepper to taste.
6. Open the air fryer and transfer the chicken tikka filling into an oven-safe dish that will fit in the lower zone of the air fryer.
7. Roll out the puff pastry sheet to fit over the top

of the dish. Place the rolled-out pastry on top of the dish, gently pressing the edges to seal. Make a few small slits on the surface of the pastry to allow steam to escape.

8. Brush the surface of the pastry with the beaten egg to create a golden crust.

9. Open the air fryer and place the dish with the chicken tikka pie in the lower zone. Close the air fryer and set the timer for 30-35 minutes to bake the pie, or until the pastry is golden and crisp.

10. Once the pastry is cooked and golden, remove the chicken tikka pie from the air fryer and let it cool for a few minutes before serving.

Beef and Stilton Pie

Prep Time: 20 minutes
Cook Time: 1 hour 30 minutes
Servings: 4
Ninja Dual Zone mode: Air Roast

Ingredients:
For the filling:
- 1.5 pounds beef stew meat, cubed
- 2 tablespoons all-purpose flour
- Salt and pepper, to taste
- 2 tablespoons vegetable oil
- 1 onion, finely chopped
- 2 cloves garlic, minced
- 2 carrots, peeled and diced
- 1 celery stalk, diced
- 2 tablespoons tomato paste
- 240g beef broth
- 120ml red wine (optional)
- 1 tablespoon Worcestershire sauce
- 1 teaspoon dried thyme
- 1 teaspoon dried rosemary
- 113g Stilton cheese, crumbled

For the pastry:
- 1 sheet puff pastry, thawed
- 1 egg, beaten (for egg wash)

Instructions:
1. Preheat the Ninja Dual Zone air fryer to 190°C in Air Roast mode.

2. In a bowl, combine the cubed beef, flour, salt, and pepper. Toss to coat the beef in the flour mixture.

3. In a large skillet, heat the vegetable oil over medium heat. Add the coated beef cubes and brown them on all sides. Remove the beef from the skillet and set aside.

4. In the same skillet, add the chopped onion, minced garlic, diced carrots, and celery. Cook until the vegetables are softened.

5. Return the browned beef cubes to the skillet with the vegetables. Stir in the tomato paste, beef broth, red wine (if using), Worcestershire sauce, dried thyme, and dried rosemary. Bring the mixture to a simmer, then reduce the heat and cover. Let it cook for about 1 hour, or until the beef is tender and the flavours are well combined.

6. Open the air fryer and transfer the beef filling into an oven-safe dish that will fit in the lower zone of the air fryer. Sprinkle the crumbled Stilton cheese evenly over the beef filling.

7. Roll out the puff pastry sheet to fit over the top of the dish. Place the rolled-out pastry on top of the dish, gently pressing the edges to seal. Make a few small slits on the surface of the pastry to allow steam to escape.

8. Brush the surface of the pastry with the beaten egg to create a golden crust.

9. Open the air fryer and place the dish with the beef and Stilton pie in the lower zone. Close the air fryer and set the timer for 30-35 minutes to bake the pie, or until the pastry is golden and crisp.

10. Once the pastry is cooked and golden, remove the beef and Stilton pie from the air fryer and let it cool for a few minutes before serving.

Chicken Tikka Masala

Prep Time: 20 minutes
Marinating time: 1 hour (optional)
Cook Time: 30 minutes
Servings: 4
Ninja Dual Zone mode: Air Roast

Ingredients:
For the chicken marinade:
- 1.5 pounds boneless, skinless chicken breasts, cut into bite-sized pieces
- 240ml plain yoghourt
- 2 tablespoons lemon juice
- 2 teaspoons ground cumin
- 2 teaspoons ground coriander
- 1 teaspoon paprika
- 1 teaspoon turmeric
- 1 teaspoon garam masala
- 1/2 teaspoon chili powder
- 1 teaspoon salt

- 1/2 teaspoon black pepper

For the tikka masala sauce:
- 2 tablespoons vegetable oil
- 1 onion, finely chopped
- 3 cloves garlic, minced
- 1-inch piece ginger, grated
- 2 teaspoons ground cumin
- 2 teaspoons ground coriander
- 2 teaspoons paprika
- 1 teaspoon turmeric
- 1 teaspoon garam masala
- 1/2 teaspoon chili powder (adjust to taste)
- 1 can crushed tomatoes
- 240g heavy cream
- 1 tablespoon tomato paste
- 1 tablespoon honey (optional, for sweetness)
- Salt, to taste
- Fresh cilantro, for garnish
- Cooked rice or naan bread, for serving

Instructions:

1. Preheat the Ninja Dual Zone air fryer to 190°C in Air Roast mode.
2. In a bowl, combine the yogurt, lemon juice, ground cumin, ground coriander, paprika, turmeric, garam masala, chili powder, salt, and black pepper. Add the chicken pieces to the marinade and toss to coat. Let it marinate in the refrigerator for at least 1 hour (or overnight for best results).
3. In a large skillet, heat the vegetable oil over medium heat. Add the chopped onion and cook until softened and translucent. Add the minced garlic and grated ginger, and cook for an additional minute.
4. In a small bowl, mix together the ground cumin, ground coriander, paprika, turmeric, garam masala, and chili powder. Add the spice mixture to the skillet and cook for about 1 minute, stirring constantly to toast the spices.
5. Stir in the crushed tomatoes, heavy cream, tomato paste, and honey (if using). Simmer the sauce for about 10 minutes, stirring occasionally, until it thickens slightly. Season with salt to taste.
6. While the sauce is simmering, arrange the marinated chicken pieces on the lower zone of the air fryer. Close the air fryer and set the timer for 15 minutes to cook the chicken.

7. After 15 minutes, open the air fryer and carefully transfer the cooked chicken pieces into the skillet with the tikka masala sauce. Stir to coat the chicken evenly with the sauce.
8. Open the air fryer and place the skillet with the chicken and sauce in the lower zone. Close the air fryer and set the timer for another 10-15 minutes to allow the flavours to meld together.
9. Once the chicken tikka masala is done, open the air fryer and give it a final stir. Garnish with fresh cilantro.

Jellied Eels

Prep Time: 30 minutes
Cook Time: 2 hours
Chilling time: 4-6 hours
Servings: 4
Ninja Dual Zone mode: Broil
Ingredients:
- 2 pounds eels, cleaned and chopped into small pieces
- 950g fish stock
- 1 onion, chopped
- 2 cloves garlic, minced
- 2 bay leaves
- 1 teaspoon salt
- 1/2 teaspoon ground black pepper
- 1/2 teaspoon ground mace
- 1/2 teaspoon ground nutmeg
- 1/4 teaspoon ground cloves
- 1/4 teaspoon ground allspice
- 1/4 teaspoon ground cinnamon
- 60ml white vinegar
- 2 tablespoons gelatin powder
- Fresh parsley, for garnish
- Lemon wedges, for serving

Instructions:

1. Preheat the Ninja Dual Zone air fryer to 95°C in Broil mode .
2. In a large saucepan, combine the fish stock, chopped onion, minced garlic, bay leaves, salt, black pepper, mace, nutmeg, cloves, allspice, and cinnamon. Bring the mixture to a simmer over medium heat.
3. Add the chopped eels to the simmering stock. Cook for about 10 minutes, until the eels are tender.
4. Using a slotted spoon, remove the cooked eels from the stock and transfer them to a dish. Discard the bay leaves. Allow the stock to cool slightly.

5. Strain the stock through a fine-mesh sieve, discarding any solids. Return the strained stock to the saucepan and add the white vinegar. Heat the stock over low heat until warm.

6. In a separate small bowl, dissolve the gelatin powder in 60ml of cold water. Let it sit for a few minutes until the gelatin absorbs the water.

7. Add the dissolved gelatin to the warm stock, stirring well to combine. Continue to heat the stock, stirring occasionally, until the gelatin is completely dissolved.

8. Open the air fryer and carefully pour the stock mixture into an oven-safe dish that will fit in the lower zone of the air fryer. Cover the dish with foil.

9. Place the covered dish in the lower zone of the air fryer. Close the air fryer and set the timer for 2 hours to slow cook the jellied eels.

10. After 2 hours, remove the dish from the air fryer and let it cool to room temperature. Once cooled, refrigerate the dish for 4-6 hours, or overnight, until the stock sets and forms a jelly-like consistency.

11. To serve, remove the dish from the refrigerator and cut the jellied eels into portions. Garnish with fresh parsley and serve with lemon wedges on the side.

Eel Pie

Prep Time: 30 minutes
Cook Time: 1 hour 30 minutes
Servings: 4
Ninja Dual Zone mode: Air Roast

Ingredients:
For the filling:
- 2 pounds eels, cleaned and cut into small pieces
- 2 tablespoons all-purpose flour
- Salt and pepper, to taste
- 2 tablespoons vegetable oil
- 1 onion, chopped
- 2 carrots, peeled and diced
- 2 celery stalks, diced
- 2 cloves garlic, minced
- 2 tablespoons tomato paste
- 480g fish stock
- 240ml white wine (optional)
- 2 bay leaves
- 1 teaspoon dried thyme
- 1 teaspoon dried rosemary

For the pastry:
- 2 sheets puff pastry, thawed
- 1 egg, beaten (for egg wash)

Instructions:
1. Preheat the Ninja Dual Zone air fryer to 190°C in Air Roast mode.

2. In a bowl, combine the all-purpose flour, salt, and pepper. Toss the eel pieces in the flour mixture to coat them evenly.

3. In a large skillet, heat the vegetable oil over medium heat. Add the floured eel pieces and brown them on all sides. Remove the eel from the skillet and set aside.

4. In the same skillet, add the chopped onion, diced carrots, diced celery, and minced garlic. Cook until the vegetables are softened.

5. Stir in the tomato paste and cook for an additional minute.

6. Return the browned eel pieces to the skillet with the vegetables. Add the fish stock, white wine (if using), bay leaves, dried thyme, and dried rosemary. Bring the mixture to a simmer, then reduce the heat and cover. Let it cook for about 1 hour, or until the eel is tender and the flavours have melded together.

7. Open the air fryer and transfer the cooked eel filling into an oven-safe dish that will fit in the lower zone of the air fryer.

8. Roll out one sheet of puff pastry to fit over the top of the dish. Place the rolled-out pastry on top of the dish, gently pressing the edges to seal. Make a few small slits on the surface of the pastry to allow steam to escape.

9. Brush the surface of the pastry with the beaten egg to create a golden crust.

10. Open the air fryer and place the dish with the eel pie in the lower zone. Close the air fryer and set the timer for 30-35 minutes to bake the pie, or until the pastry is golden and crisp.

11. Once the pastry is cooked and golden, remove the eel pie from the air fryer and let it cool for a few minutes before serving.

Stargazy Pie

Prep Time: 30 minutes
Cook Time: 1 hour
Servings: 4
Ninja Dual Zone mode: Air Roast

Ingredients:
- 2 pounds whole herrings, cleaned and filleted
- 4 tablespoons butter, divided
- 1 onion, finely chopped
- 2 cloves garlic, minced
- 2 tablespoons all-purpose flour
- 240g fish stock
- 120ml white wine (optional)
- 240g heavy cream
- 1 tablespoon lemon juice
- Salt and pepper, to taste
- 4 hard-boiled eggs, halved
- 1 sheet puff pastry, thawed
- 1 egg, beaten (for egg wash)

Instructions:
1. Preheat the Ninja Dual Zone air fryer to 190°C in Air Roast mode.
2. Rinse the herrings under cold water and pat them dry with paper towels. Season the herrings with salt and pepper.
3. In a large skillet, melt 2 tablespoons of butter over medium heat. Add the chopped onion and minced garlic, and cook until softened and translucent.
4. In a separate small bowl, mix the flour with a little water to make a smooth paste.
5. Add the flour paste to the skillet and cook for a minute, stirring constantly.
6. Slowly add the fish stock and white wine (if using), stirring continuously to avoid lumps.
7. Stir in the heavy cream and lemon juice. Continue to cook and stir until the sauce thickens. Season with salt and pepper to taste.
8. Open the air fryer and transfer the sauce to an oven-safe dish that will fit in the lower zone of the air fryer.
9. Arrange the herring fillets in the dish, making sure they are evenly spaced and partially submerged in the sauce.
10. Place the halved hard-boiled eggs, yolk-side up, among the herring fillets.
11. Roll out the puff pastry sheet to fit over the top of the dish. Place the rolled-out pastry on top of the dish, pressing the edges to seal. Make a small hole in the centre of the pastry to allow steam to escape.
12. Brush the surface of the pastry with the beaten egg to create a golden crust.

13. Open the air fryer and place the dish with the Stargazy Pie in the lower zone. Close the air fryer and set the timer for 45-50 minutes to bake the pie, or until the pastry is golden and crisp.
14. Once the pastry is cooked and golden, remove the Stargazy Pie from the air fryer and let it cool for a few minutes before serving.

Sussex Pond Pudding

Prep Time: 20 minutes
Cook Time: 2 hours
Servings: 6
Ninja Dual Zone mode: Air Fry

Ingredients:
- 1 large lemon
- 125g all-purpose flour
- 113g unsalted butter, softened
- 100g granulated sugar
- 1 large egg
- 1/4 teaspoon salt
- 2 tablespoons milk
- 6 tablespoons golden syrup (or light corn syrup)

Instructions:
1. Preheat the Ninja Dual Zone air fryer to 95°C in Air Fry mode.
2. Zest the lemon and set the zest aside. Cut the lemon in half and juice it.
3. In a mixing bowl, cream together the softened butter and sugar until light and fluffy.
4. Beat in the egg and lemon zest until well combined.
5. In a separate bowl, whisk together the flour and salt. Gradually add the flour mixture to the butter mixture, alternating with the milk. Mix until you have a smooth batter.
6. Grease a heatproof dish that will fit in the lower zone of the air fryer. Pour the golden syrup into the dish.
7. Take one of the lemon halves and prick it all over with a fork. Place the lemon half, pricked side down, on top of the syrup in the dish.
8. Pour the batter over the lemon half, covering it completely. Smooth the surface with a spatula.
9. Place the dish in the lower zone of the air fryer. Close the air fryer and set the timer for 2 hours to slow cook the pudding.
10. After 2 hours, carefully remove the dish from the air fryer. The pudding should be golden and set.
11. To serve, spoon some of the pudding into individual

bowls or plates, making sure to include some of the lemon-infused syrup. Serve it warm.

Scotch Broth

Prep Time: 15 minutes
Cook Time: 1 hour 30 minutes
Servings: 6
Ninja Dual Zone mode: Broil

Ingredients:

- 1 pound lamb shoulder, bone-in, trimmed of excess fat
- 1 tablespoon vegetable oil
- 1 onion, chopped
- 2 carrots, peeled and diced
- 2 celery stalks, diced
- 2 cloves garlic, minced
- 1 leek, cleaned and sliced
- 90g pearl barley
- 1420g beef or vegetable broth
- 2 sprigs fresh thyme
- 2 bay leaves
- Salt and pepper, to taste
- Chopped fresh parsley, for garnish

Instructions:

1. Preheat the Ninja Dual Zone air fryer to 95°C in Broil mode.
2. In a large skillet, heat the vegetable oil over medium-high heat. Add the lamb shoulder and brown it on all sides. Remove the lamb from the skillet and set it aside.
3. In the same skillet, add the chopped onion, diced carrots, diced celery, minced garlic, and sliced leek. Sauté until the vegetables start to soften, about 5 minutes.
4. Open the air fryer and transfer the sautéed vegetables to the lower zone of the air fryer.
5. Add the pearl barley, beef or vegetable broth, fresh thyme sprigs, and bay leaves to the air fryer.
6. Place the browned lamb shoulder on top of the vegetables and broth mixture.
7. Season with salt and pepper to taste.
8. Close the air fryer and set the timer for 1 hour and 30 minutes to slow cook the Scotch Broth.
9. After 1 hour and 30 minutes, carefully remove the lamb shoulder from the broth. Discard the bones and shred the meat using two forks. Return the shredded lamb to the broth in the air fryer.
10. Remove the thyme sprigs and bay leaves from the broth.
11. Serve the Scotch Broth hot, garnished with chopped fresh parsley.

Fisherman's Pie

Prep Time: 30 minutes
Cook Time: 30 minutes
Servings: 6
Ninja Dual Zone mode: Air Bake

Ingredients:

- 1 ½ pounds white fish fillets (such as cod or haddock), cut into bite-sized pieces
- 1 pound peeled and deveined shrimp
- 150g frozen peas
- 155g frozen corn
- 1 onion, finely chopped
- 2 cloves garlic, minced
- 2 tablespoons butter
- 2 tablespoons all-purpose flour
- 350ml milk
- 1 tablespoon Dijon mustard
- 2 tablespoons chopped fresh dill
- Salt and pepper, to taste
- 900g mashed potatoes
- Grated cheddar cheese, for topping

Instructions:

1. Preheat the Ninja Dual Zone air fryer to 190°C in Air Bake mode.
2. In a large skillet, melt the butter over medium heat. Add the chopped onion and minced garlic. Cook until the onion is softened and translucent.
3. Add the flour to the skillet and stir well to coat the onions and garlic. Cook for about a minute to cook off the raw flour taste.
4. Gradually whisk in the milk, stirring constantly to avoid lumps. Cook until the sauce thickens and comes to a simmer.
5. Stir in the Dijon mustard and chopped dill. Season with salt and pepper to taste.
6. Add the white fish fillets, shrimp, frozen peas, and frozen corn to the skillet. Gently stir to combine and coat the seafood and vegetables with the sauce.
7. Transfer the fish and seafood mixture to an oven-safe dish that will fit in the lower zone of the air fryer.
8. Spread the mashed potatoes over the top of the fish mixture, covering it completely. Smooth the surface with a spatula.

9. Open the air fryer and place the dish with the Fisherman's Pie in the lower zone. Close the air fryer and set the timer for 30 minutes to bake the pie.
10. After 30 minutes, open the air fryer and sprinkle the grated cheddar cheese over the top of the mashed potatoes.
11. Close the air fryer and continue to cook for another 5 minutes, or until the cheese is melted and golden.
12. Carefully remove the Fisherman's Pie from the air fryer and let it cool for a few minutes before serving.

Classic British Street Potato

Serves 4
Prep Time: 5 minutes / Cook Time: 50 minutes
Ingredients
- 6 large potatoes
- 100g butter
- 1 tsp ground black pepper (optional)
- 1 tsp table salt

Instructions:
1. Make multiple insertions in the potato with a fork, ensuring they do not burst whilst baking
2. Place the potatoes into both zones of the of the ninja foodi duel zone (3 in each)
3. select the 'BAKE' function at 200° for 50 minutes
4. Press 'MATCH' then 'START/STOP'
5. At the 40 minute mark cut an 'X' on the potato and insert 1 heaped tbsp of butter into the potato cavities
6. Slide the draws back into the ninja foodi duel to cook for the remainder 10 minutes
7. Retrieve the potatoes and season with salt and pepper, before serving

Cornish Yarg and Potato Pasty

Prep Time: 30 minutes
Cook Time: 40 minutes
Servings: 4
Ninja Dual Zone mode: Air Roast

Ingredients:
For the pastry:
- 310g all-purpose flour
- 1 teaspoon salt
- 227g unsalted butter, cold and cubed
- 6-8 tablespoons ice water

For the filling:
- 2 medium potatoes, peeled and diced
- 1 small onion, finely chopped
- 110g Cornish Yarg cheese, grated (or any other hard cheese of your choice)
- 1 tablespoon chopped fresh thyme
- Salt and pepper, to taste
- 1 egg, beaten (for egg wash)

Instructions:
1. Preheat the Ninja Dual Zone air fryer to 190°C in Air Roast mode.
2. In a large mixing bowl, combine the flour and salt. Add the cold, cubed butter and use a pastry cutter or your fingertips to rub the butter into the flour until the mixture resembles coarse breadcrumbs.
3. Gradually add the ice water, a tablespoon at a time, and mix until the dough comes together. Be careful not to overmix. Shape the dough into a ball, cover it with plastic wrap, and refrigerate for 30 minutes.
4. In the meantime, prepare the filling. Boil the diced potatoes in salted water until they are just tender. Drain and set aside to cool.
5. In a separate bowl, combine the cooled potatoes, chopped onion, grated Cornish Yarg cheese, chopped fresh thyme, salt, and pepper. Mix well to combine.
6. On a lightly floured surface, roll out the chilled pastry dough to a thickness of about ¼ inch (0.6 cm). Cut out rounds or rectangles of approximately 6-7 inches (15-18 cm) in diameter.
7. Place a spoonful of the filling mixture onto one half of each pastry round or rectangle, leaving a small border around the edges. Fold the other half of the pastry over the filling and press the edges together to seal. Crimp the edges with a fork to create a decorative pattern.
8. Place the pasties on a parchment-lined baking sheet that will fit in the lower zone of the air fryer.
9. Brush the pasties with the beaten egg to create a golden crust.
10. Open the air fryer and place the baking sheet with the pasties in the lower zone. Close the air fryer and set the timer for 40 minutes to bake the pasties, or until they are golden and crispy.
11. Once the pasties are cooked, carefully remove them from the air fryer and let them cool for a few minutes before serving.

Chapter 5: Appetizers

Mini Vegetable Samosas

Serves: 6-8
Prep Time: 30 minutes
Cook Time: 15-20 minutes
Ninja Dual Zone mode: Air Fry

Ingredients:
- 128g frozen mixed vegetables
- 64g diced onion
- 2 garlic cloves, minced
- 1 tsp grated ginger
- 1 tsp cumin powder
- 1 tsp coriander powder
- 1/2 tsp turmeric powder
- Salt and pepper to taste
- 1 tbsp vegetable oil
- 12-15 mini samosa pastry sheets

Instructions:
1. Preheat the Ninja Dual Zone to Air Fry at 200°C.
2. In a skillet, heat the vegetable oil over medium heat.
3. Add the onion, garlic, and ginger and sauté for 2-3 minutes until the onion is translucent.
4. Add the frozen mixed vegetables, cumin powder, coriander powder, turmeric powder, salt, and pepper. Cook for 5-7 minutes until the vegetables are tender.
5. Remove the skillet from heat and allow the mixture to cool.
6. Cut the samosa pastry sheets into small triangles and fill each triangle with a spoonful of the vegetable mixture.
7. Place the samosas in the air fryer basket and Air Fry at 200°C for 10-12 minutes until they are crispy and golden brown.

Cauliflower Buffalo Bites

Serves: 4-6
Prep Time: 10 minutes
Cook Time: 10-12 minutes
Ninja Dual Zone mode: Air Fry

Ingredients:
- 1 head of cauliflower, cut into small florets
- 64g all-purpose flour
- 1 tsp garlic powder
- 1/2 tsp smoked paprika
- 1/2 tsp salt
- 1/2 tsp black pepper
- 64g buffalo sauce
- 2 tbsp melted butter

Instructions:
1. Preheat the Ninja Dual Zone to Air Fry at 190°C.
2. In a bowl, mix the flour, garlic powder, smoked paprika, salt, and black pepper.
3. Add the cauliflower florets to the bowl and toss until they are coated in the flour mixture.
4. Place the cauliflower in the air fryer basket and Air Fry at 190°C for 10-12 minutes until they are crispy and golden brown.
5. In a separate bowl, mix the buffalo sauce and melted butter.
6. Toss the cooked cauliflower in the buffalo sauce mixture until they are coated.
7. Serve hot.

Mini Cornish Pasties

Serves: 6-8
Prep Time: 30 minutes
Cook Time: 25-30 minutes
Ninja Dual Zone mode: Air Fry

Ingredients:
- 320g of all-purpose flour
- 1/2 tsp salt
- 1/2 tsp baking powder
- 64g unsalted butter, chilled and diced
- 64g vegetable shortening, chilled and diced
- 60 ml of cold water
- 1 egg, beaten
- 1 large potato, peeled and diced
- 1 large carrot, peeled and diced
- 1 small onion, peeled and diced
- 128g cooked diced beef
- Salt and pepper, to taste
- 1 tbsp butter, diced

Instructions:
1. Preheat your Ninja Dual Zone to 190°C (190°C) on Air Fry mode.
2. In a large bowl, whisk together flour, salt, and baking powder. Using a pastry blender, cut in

butter and shorten until the mixture resembles coarse crumbs.

3. Add cold water and stir until a dough forms. Turn out onto a floured surface and knead for 1-2 minutes until smooth. Divide dough into 8 equal portions and roll each into a ball.

4. In a separate bowl, combine diced potato, carrot, onion, and cooked beef. Season with salt and pepper to taste.

5. On a floured surface, roll each ball of dough into a 5-inch circle. Spoon 32g of the beef and vegetable mixture onto one half of each circle. Dot with butter.

6. Fold the other half of the dough over the filling and crimp the edges together to seal. Brush the beaten egg over the pasties.

7. Place the pasties in the Ninja Dual Zone on Air Fry mode for 18-20 minutes or until golden brown and crispy.

Potted shrimp

Serves: 4-6
Prep Time: 15 minutes
Cook Time: 5-7 minutes
Ninja Dual Zone mode: Air Fry

Ingredients:
- 250g unsalted butter, softened
- 500g cooked and peeled shrimp
- 1 small shallot, finely chopped
- 1 garlic clove, minced
- 1 tsp ground mace
- 1/2 tsp ground nutmeg
- 1/2 tsp cayenne pepper
- Juice of 1/2 lemon
- Salt and black pepper to taste

Instructions:
1. Preheat your Ninja Dual Zone to the "Air Fry" mode at 177°C (177°C).

2. Melt 2 tbsp of the butter in a frying pan over medium heat. Add the shallot and garlic and sauté until softened.

3. Add the shrimp to the frying pan and cook for 2-3 minutes, stirring occasionally.

4. Remove the frying pan from the heat and stir in the mace, nutmeg, cayenne pepper, lemon juice, and the remaining butter. Mix well until the butter is melted and everything is well combined.

5. Season with salt and black pepper to taste.

6. Spoon the mixture into small ramekins or jars and pack down lightly.

7. Place the ramekins or jars into the Ninja Dual Zone basket and air fry for 5-7 minutes, until the butter on top of the pots is melted and bubbling.

8. Remove from the Ninja Dual Zone and let cool to room temperature before serving.

Miniature pork pies

Serves: 4-6
Prep Time: 20 minutes
Cook Time: 12-15 minutes
Ninja Dual Zone mode: Air Fry

Ingredients:
- 250g ground pork
- 1/2 onion, finely chopped
- 1 tsp dried sage
- 1/2 tsp salt
- 1/4 tsp black pepper
- 1 egg, beaten
- 2 sheets of pre-made pie crust

Instructions:
1. Preheat your Ninja Dual Zone to 190°C on the Air Fryer mode.

2. In a mixing bowl, combine the ground pork, chopped onion, dried sage, salt, and black pepper.

3. Roll out the pie crust sheets and use a round cookie cutter to cut out circles (about 3-4 inches in diameter).

4. Add about 1 tablespoon of the pork mixture onto each circle of pie crust.

5. Fold the edges of the crust up and over the filling, pinching the edges together to create a seal.

6. Brush the beaten egg over the tops of the pork pies.

7. Place the pork pies into the Air Fryer basket and air fry for 12-15 minutes, or until golden brown and cooked through.

Crispy black pudding bites

Serves: 4-6
Prep Time: 15 minutes
Cook Time: 6-8 minutes
Ninja Dual Zone mode: Air Fryer

Ingredients:
- 250g black pudding, sliced into rounds
- 64g flour

- 1 tsp paprika
- 1/2 tsp garlic powder
- 1/4 tsp salt
- 1/4 tsp black pepper
- 1 egg, beaten
- 128g panko breadcrumbs

Instructions:

1. Preheat your Ninja Dual Zone to 200°C on the Air Fryer mode.
2. In a small mixing bowl, combine the flour, paprika, garlic powder, salt, and black pepper.
3. Dip each slice of black pudding into the flour mixture, shaking off any excess.
4. Dip the floured black pudding slices into the beaten egg, then coat with the panko breadcrumbs.
5. Place the black pudding bites into the Air Fryer basket and air fry for 6-8 minutes, or until crispy and golden brown.

Smoked salmon pate

Serves: 4-6
Prep Time: 10 minutes
Cook Time: 0 minutes
Ninja Dual Zone mode: Air Fry

Ingredients:

- 226g smoked salmon, roughly chopped
- 113g cream cheese, softened
- 2 tbsp mayonnaise
- 2 tbsp sour cream
- 1 tbsp freshly squeezed lemon juice
- 1 tsp Dijon mustard
- 1/4 tsp salt
- 1/8 tsp black pepper
- Chives or dill, for garnish

Instructions:

1. In a food processor, combine the smoked salmon, cream cheese, mayonnaise, sour cream, lemon juice, Dijon mustard, salt, and black pepper.
2. Pulse the Ingredients together until they are well combined and the mixture is smooth.
3. Transfer the smoked salmon pate to a serving dish, cover, and refrigerate for at least 30 minutes or until ready to serve.
4. Garnish with chives or dill before serving.

Baked goat cheese with honey and walnuts

Serves: 4-6
Prep Time: 5 minutes
Cook Time: 10 minutes
Ninja Dual Zone mode: Air Fry

Ingredients:

- 226g goat cheese
- 32g honey
- 32g chopped walnuts
- Crackers or baguette slices, for serving

Instructions:

1. Preheat the Ninja Dual Zone to 190°C on Air Fry mode.
2. In a small bowl, combine the honey and chopped walnuts.
3. Roll the goat cheese into small balls or shape it into a log.
4. Dip the goat cheese into the honey and walnut mixture, coating it evenly.
5. Place the coated goat cheese onto a baking sheet lined with parchment paper.
6. Air fry the goat cheese for 10 minutes, or until the cheese is soft and slightly golden.
7. Serve the baked goat cheese with crackers or baguette slices.

Mini Yorkshire puddings with roast beef and horseradish sauce

Serves: 12
Prep Time: 10 minutes
Cook Time: 15 minutes
Ninja Dual Zone mode: Air Fry

Ingredients:

- 64g all-purpose flour
- 64g milk
- 2 eggs
- Salt and pepper, to taste
- 125g roast beef, thinly sliced
- 32g sour cream
- 2 tablespoons prepared horseradish
- Fresh chives, chopped

Instructions:

1. Preheat the Ninja Dual Zone to Air Fry mode at 190°C.
2. In a mixing bowl, whisk together the flour, milk,

eggs, salt, and pepper until well combined.

3. Pour the batter into a greased mini muffin tin, filling each cup about 3/4 of the way full.

4. Air fry the Yorkshire puddings for 10-12 minutes or until puffed and golden brown.

5. In a small bowl, mix the sour cream and horseradish until smooth.

6. Once the Yorkshire puddings are done, let them cool for a few minutes and then slice off the top and add a slice of roast beef to each one.

7. Spoon a dollop of horseradish cream on top of the roast beef and sprinkle with chopped chives.

8. Serve while still hot and enjoy.

Mini quiches with bacon and cheddar

Serves: 12
Prep Time: 10 minutes
Cook Time: 15 minutes
Ninja Dual Zone mode: Bake

Ingredients:

- 64g milk
- 2 eggs
- Salt and pepper, to taste
- 64g cooked bacon, crumbled
- 64g shredded cheddar cheese
- 2 tablespoons chopped fresh parsley
- 12 mini tart shells (store-bought or homemade)

Instructions:

1. Preheat the Ninja Dual Zone to Bake mode at 190°C.

2. In a mixing bowl, whisk together the milk, eggs, salt, and pepper until well combined.

3. Stir in the bacon, cheddar cheese, and parsley.

4. Arrange the mini tart shells on a baking sheet and fill each one with the egg mixture.

5. Bake the mini quiches for 12-15 minutes or until the filling is set and the crust is golden brown.

6. Let the quiches cool for a few minutes before removing them from the tart shells.

7. Serve and enjoy!

Sausage rolls

Serves: 12
Prep Time: 10 minutes
Cook Time: 15-20 minutes
Ninja Dual Zone mode: Air Fry

Ingredients:

- 1 sheet puff pastry, thawed
- 6 pork sausages, casings removed
- 1 egg, beaten
- Sesame seeds (optional)

Instructions:

1. Preheat the Ninja Dual Zone to Air Fry mode at 190°C.

2. Roll out the puff pastry sheet into a rectangle, then cut it in half lengthwise.

3. Divide the sausage meat into 6 portions and roll each one into a sausage shape.

4. Place a sausage on each piece of pastry, then fold the pastry over the sausage and seal the edges.

5. Cut each pastry roll into two or three pieces, depending on how big you want your sausage rolls to be.

6. Brush the tops of the sausage rolls with beaten egg and sprinkle with sesame seeds (optional).

7. Place the sausage rolls in the Air Fryer basket and air fry for 15-20 minutes or until golden brown and cooked through.

8. Let the sausage rolls cool for a few minutes before serving.

Crispy duck spring rolls

Serves: 4
Prep Time: 20 minutes
Cook Time: 10 minutes
Ninja Dual Zone mode: Air Fry

Ingredients:

- 1 package of spring roll wrappers
- 1 duck breast, cooked and shredded
- 128g shredded cabbage
- 128g shredded carrots
- 64g sliced green onions
- 2 cloves garlic, minced
- 1 tablespoon soy sauce
- 1 tablespoon hoisin sauce
- 1 tablespoon rice vinegar
- 1 tablespoon cornstarch
- 1 tablespoon water
- Vegetable oil for brushing

Instructions:

1. In a bowl, mix the shredded duck, cabbage, carrots, green onions, garlic, soy sauce, hoisin sauce, and rice vinegar.

2. In a small bowl, whisk together the cornstarch and water to make a slurry.
3. Lay out a spring roll wrapper and place a spoonful of the duck mixture in the centre.
4. Roll the wrapper around the filling, tucking in the sides as you go.
5. Brush the spring rolls with vegetable oil.
6. Place the spring rolls in the air fryer basket, making sure they are not touching.
7. Air fry at 190°C for 8-10 minutes, or until crispy and golden brown.
8. Serve with a dipping sauce of your choice.

Deviled eggs

Serves: 3
Prep Time: 10 minutes
Cook Time: 8 minutes
Ninja Dual Zone mode: Air Fry

Ingredients:
- 6 hard-boiled eggs
- 32g mayonnaise
- 1 tablespoon Dijon mustard
- 1/4 teaspoon garlic powder
- Salt and pepper to taste
- Paprika for garnish

Instructions:
1. Cut the hard-boiled eggs in half lengthwise and remove the yolks.
2. In a bowl, mix the egg yolks, mayonnaise, dijon mustard, garlic powder, salt, and pepper until smooth.
3. Spoon the mixture into the egg white halves.
4. Place the deviled eggs in the air fryer basket, making sure they are not touching.
5. Air fry at 165°C for 6-8 minutes, or until heated through.
6. Garnish with paprika and serve.

Stilton-stuffed mushrooms

Serves: 4
Prep Time: 15 minutes
Cook Time: 12 minutes
Ninja Dual Zone mode: Air Fry

Ingredients:
- 12 large mushrooms, stems removed
- 113g cream cheese, softened
- 32g crumbled Stilton cheese
- 1 clove garlic, minced
- 1 tablespoon chopped fresh parsley
- Salt and pepper to taste
- 32g bread crumbs
- 1 tablespoon olive oil

Instructions:
1. In a bowl, mix the cream cheese, stilton cheese, garlic, parsley, salt, and pepper.
2. Stuff each mushroom cap with the cheese mixture.
3. In a separate bowl, mix the bread crumbs and olive oil.
4. Dip each mushroom cap in the breadcrumb mixture to coat.
5. Place the mushrooms in the air fryer basket, making sure they are not touching.
6. Air fry at 190°C for 10-12 minutes, or until the mushrooms are tender and the bread crumbs are golden brown.
7. Serve hot.

Caprese Skewers

Serves: 4
Prep Time: 10 minutes
Cook Time: 10 minutes
Ninja Dual Zone mode: Air Fry

Ingredients:
- Cherry tomatoes
- Fresh basil leaves
- Mini mozzarella balls
- Balsamic glaze
- Salt and pepper
- Skewers

Instructions:
1. Preheat the Ninja Dual Zone to 190°C using the Air Fry mode.
2. Assemble the skewers by threading a cherry tomato, a basil leaf, and a mini mozzarella ball onto each skewer. Repeat until all Ingredients are used up.
3. Season the skewers with salt and pepper to taste.
4. Place the skewers in the basket of the Ninja Dual Zone Ninja Dual .
5. Air fry the skewers for 10 minutes or until the cheese is melted and the tomatoes are slightly softened.
6. Drizzle balsamic glaze over the skewers before serving.

Breaded whitebait

Serves: 4
Prep Time: 15 minutes
Cook Time: 6-8 minutes
Ninja Dual Zone mode: Air Fry

Ingredients:

- 500g fresh whitebait
- 64g all-purpose flour
- 1 tsp paprika
- 1 tsp garlic powder
- Salt and pepper, to taste
- 1 egg, beaten
- 164g breadcrumbs

Instructions:

1. Preheat the Ninja Dual Zone to 200°C (200°C).
2. In a bowl, mix the flour, paprika, garlic powder, salt, and pepper.
3. Dip the white bait in the beaten egg, then dredge them in the flour mixture.
4. Roll the whitebait in breadcrumbs to coat.
5. Place the white bait in the air fryer basket and cook for 6-8 minutes until golden brown and crispy.

Fried pickles with dipping sauce

Serves: 4
Prep Time: 15 minutes
Cook Time: 8-10 minutes
Ninja Dual Zone mode: Air Fry

Ingredients:

- 128g all-purpose flour
- 1 tsp paprika
- 1 tsp garlic powder
- Salt and pepper, to taste
- 128g buttermilk
- 64g panko breadcrumbs
- 64g cornmeal
- 64g grated Parmesan cheese
- 1 jar dill pickles, drained and sliced
- Vegetable oil, for frying
- Dipping sauce (ranch, honey mustard, or your preferred sauce)

Instructions:

1. Preheat the Ninja Dual Zone to 190°C (190°C).
2. In a bowl, mix the flour, paprika, garlic powder, salt, and pepper.
3. In a separate bowl, pour the buttermilk.
4. In another bowl, mix the panko breadcrumbs, cornmeal, and Parmesan cheese.
5. Dip the pickle slices in the flour mixture, then in the buttermilk, and then in the breadcrumb mixture.
6. Place the breaded pickles in the air fryer basket and spray them with cooking spray.
7. Cook for 8-10 minutes, shaking the basket halfway through, until golden brown and crispy.
8. Serve the fried pickles with dipping sauce.

Spinach and Feta Filo Triangles

Serves: 4
Prep Time: 15 minutes
Cook Time: 10-12 minutes
Ninja Dual Zone mode: Air Fry

Ingredients:

- 256 of chopped fresh spinach
- 64g crumbled feta cheese
- 32g grated parmesan cheese
- 2 tablespoons chopped fresh dill
- 1/4 teaspoon salt
- 1/4 teaspoon black pepper
- 1/4 teaspoon garlic powder
- 8 sheets of phyllo dough
- 32g unsalted butter, melted

Instructions:

1. Preheat the Ninja Dual Zone to 190°C in air fryer mode.
2. In a mixing bowl, combine chopped spinach, feta cheese, parmesan cheese, dill, salt, black pepper, and garlic powder. Mix well.
3. Place a sheet of phyllo dough on a flat surface and brush with melted butter. Add another sheet of phyllo dough on top and brush with melted butter. Repeat until 4 sheets have been used.
4. Cut the phyllo dough into 8 equal triangles.
5. Place 1 tablespoon of the spinach and feta mixture on the wide end of each triangle.
6. Roll the dough over the mixture to form a triangle shape.
7. Brush the outside of the triangles with melted butter.
8. Place the triangles in the air fryer basket and cook for 10-12 minutes or until golden brown and crispy.
9. Serve hot.

Garlic and herb-stuffed olives

Serves: 4
Prep Time: 10 minutes
Cook Time: 5-6 minutes
Ninja Dual Zone mode: Air Fry

Ingredients:
- 128g green olives, pitted
- 2 garlic cloves, minced
- 1 tablespoon chopped fresh parsley
- 1 tablespoon chopped fresh oregano
- 1 tablespoon olive oil

Instructions:
1. Preheat the Ninja Dual Zone to 177°C in air fryer mode.
2. In a small mixing bowl, combine the pitted green olives, minced garlic, chopped parsley, chopped oregano, and olive oil. Mix well.
3. Stuff the garlic and herb mixture into the centre of each olive.
4. Place the stuffed olives in the air fryer basket and cook for 5-6 minutes or until heated through and slightly crispy.
5. Serve hot.

Autumn Oat Bake

Prep Time: 10 minutes
Cook Time: 20 minutes
Serves: 7
Ninja Dual Zone mode: Bake

Ingredients
- 400g old-fashioned oats
- 2 tsp coconut oil, melted
- 2 small eggs, beaten
- 360ml full-fat coconut milk
- 2 small apples, cored, peeled, and sliced
- 1 tsp baking powder
- 170 honey
- A pinch of ground cinnamon
- 1 tsp vanilla bean paste
- A pinch of grated nutmeg

Instructions:
1. Brush the inside of two oven-safe baking tins with coconut oil. Thoroughly combine all the Ingredients and spoon the mixture into the baking tins.
2. Select zone 1 and pair it with "BAKE" at 190°C for 20 minutes. Select "MATCH" to duplicate

settings across both zones. Press the "START/STOP" button.
3. When zone 1 time reaches 10 minutes, turn the baking tins and reinsert the drawers to continue cooking.

Sweet & Salty Popcorn

Prep Time: 30minutes
Cook Time: 20 minutes
Serves: 4
Ninja Dual Zone mode: Air Fry

Ingredients
- 100g raw popcorn kernels
- 1cal olive oil spray
- ½ tsp salt
- 1 tbs sugar

Instructions:
1. Line both zone draws with the crisper plates
2. Place 50g of kernels in each zone draw
3. Spray the kernels with olive oil and dash salt and sugar
4. Select the zones, pairing with 'AIR FRY' at 200°C for 15 minutes
5. Press 'MATCH' then 'START/STOP' to begin popping through kernels
6. Retrieve the popcorn, and then pile it up into a share bowl sprinkle salt and shake

Butter-Fried Asparagus

Prep Time: 10minutes
Cook Time: 15 minutes
Serves: 5
Ninja Dual Zone mode: Air Fry

Ingredients
- 1kg asparagus spears, trimmed
- 2 tbsp butter, melted
- 2 garlic cloves, pressed
- 1 tsp dried dill weed
- 1 tsp paprika
- Sea salt and ground black pepper, to taste
- 1/2 lemon, juiced and zested

Instructions:
1. In a mixing dish, toss asparagus with the other Ingredients until well coated in butter and aromatics.
2. Add asparagus to both drawers of your Ninja Foodi (with a crisper plate inserted).

3. Select zone 1 and pair it with "AIR FRY" at 200°C for 15 minutes. Select "MATCH" followed by the "START/STOP" button.
4. At the halfway point, stir the Ingredients to ensure even cooking; reinsert the drawers to resume cooking

Mixed Berry Crisp

Prep Time: 5minutes
Cook Time: 35 minutes
Serves: 6
Ninja Dual Zone mode: Bake

Ingredients

- 200g mixed berries, fresh or frozen (and thawed)
- 1 tsp fresh ginger, peeled and minced
- 1 tbsp cornstarch
- 50g golden caster sugar
- 100g old-fashioned rolled oats
- 100g coconut oil, at room temperature
- 50g honey
- 1/2 tsp ground cinnamon
- 1 tsp vanilla bean paste
- 120g walnuts, finely chopped

Instructions:

1. Spray the inside of a baking tin with nonstick cooking oil.
2. Toss the mixed berries with ginger, cornstarch, and caster sugar. Arrange the mixed berries in the baking tin.
3. In a mixing dish, thoroughly combine all the topping Ingredients. Place the topping mixture over the mixed berry layer.
4. Add the baking tin to the zone 1 drawer.
5. Select zone 1 and pair it with "BAKE" at 165°C for 35 minutes. Press the "START/STOP" button.

Extra Crispy Sausage Patties With Avocado Slices

Prep Time: 5 minutes
Cook Time: 8 minutes
Serves: 12
Ninja Dual Zone mode: Air Fry
Prep Time: 5 minutes / Cook Time: 8 minutes

Ingredients

- 500g fresh Sausage Patties
- 2 tbsp olive oil
- 50g sesame seeds
- 1 Avocado, peeled

Instructions:

1. Slice the sausage patties, brush them with oil, followed by topping them with some sesame seeds
2. Preheat the air fryer unit to 180°C for 3 minutes
3. Divide the patties and place them in the draws of the dual zone air fryer
4. Pair the zones to 'AIR FRY' at 180°C for 5 minutes
5. Press 'MATCH' followed by 'STOP/START' to caramelise the pineapple
6. Flip the sausage patties at the halfway point of cooking
7. Slice the avocado into 12 pieces
8. Retrieve the sausage patties and then serve with the avocado slices

Chapter 6: Desserts

Apple Crumble

Serves: 4-6
Prep Time: 15 minutes
Cook Time: 12-15 minutes
Ninja Dual Zone mode: Air Fry

Ingredients:
- 500g of peeled, cored, and sliced apples
- 64g all-purpose flour
- 64g rolled oats
- 64g brown sugar
- 32g unsalted butter, chilled and cut into small pieces
- 1/2 teaspoon ground cinnamon
- 1/4 teaspoon ground nutmeg

Instructions:
1. Preheat your Ninja Dual Zone to Air Fry mode at 190°C for 5 minutes.
2. In a mixing bowl, combine flour, rolled oats, brown sugar, butter, cinnamon, and nutmeg. Use a pastry blender or your fingers to mix the Ingredients until the mixture resembles coarse crumbs.
3. Place the sliced apples in a baking dish and spread the crumble mixture on top.
4. Air Fry for 12-15 minutes or until the top is golden brown and the apples are soft and tender.
5. Let cool for a few minutes and serve warm.

Banoffee Pie

Serves: 6-8
Prep Time: 20 minutes
Cook Time: 10-12 minutes
Ninja Dual Zone mode: Bake

Ingredients:
- 1 pie crust
- 3 ripe bananas, sliced
- 64g heavy cream
- 64g sweetened condensed milk
- 1 tablespoon butter
- 1/2 teaspoon vanilla extract
- Whipped cream and chocolate shavings for topping (optional)

Instructions:
1. Preheat your Ninja Dual Zone to Bake mode at 177°C for 5 minutes.

2. In a saucepan, melt the butter over low heat. Add sweetened condensed milk and cook, stirring constantly, until the mixture thickens and turns caramel-coloured, about 10-15 minutes.
3. Remove the pan from the heat and add the vanilla extract. Let cool for a few minutes.
4. Spread the sliced bananas at the bottom of the pie crust. Pour the caramel mixture over the bananas and spread it evenly.
5. Bake for 10-12 minutes or until the edges of the pie crust are golden brown.
6. Let cool for a few minutes and refrigerate for at least 30 minutes or until the filling sets.
7. Top with whipped cream and chocolate shavings (optional) and serve.

Bread and Butter Pudding

Serves: 4-6
Prep Time: 15 minutes
Cook Time: 20 minutes
Ninja Dual Zone mode: Air Fry

Ingredients:
- 6 slices of white bread
- 50g unsalted butter, softened
- 50g raisins
- 2 large eggs
- 350ml whole milk
- 50g caster sugar
- 1 tsp vanilla extract
- 1/2 tsp ground cinnamon
- Pinch of nutmeg

Instructions:
1. Preheat the Ninja Dual Zone to 177°C on air fry mode.
2. Butter the bread and cut it into quarters. Layer the bread and raisins in a 20cm baking dish.
3. In a mixing bowl, whisk together the eggs, milk, sugar, vanilla extract, cinnamon, and nutmeg.
4. Pour the mixture over the bread and raisins, making sure all the bread is covered.
5. Place the baking dish in the Ninja Dual Zone and cook for 20 minutes or until the top is golden brown.
6. Serve warm with a dollop of whipped cream or custard.

Chocolate Eclairs

Serves: 6-8
Prep Time: 30 minutes
Cook Time: 20 minutes
Ninja Dual Zone mode:
Bake

Ingredients:
For the choux pastry:
- 60g unsalted butter, cut into small pieces
- 75g plain flour
- 2 large eggs
- 120ml water
- For the filling:
- 300ml double cream
- 50g caster sugar
- 1 tsp vanilla extract
- 100g dark chocolate, chopped

For the icing:
- 100g icing sugar
- 2 tbsp cocoa powder
- 2-3 tbsp hot water

Instructions:
1. Preheat the Ninja Dual Zone to 200°C on bake mode.
2. To make the choux pastry, place the butter and water in a saucepan and heat until the butter has melted. Bring to a boil, then remove from the heat and add the flour. Stir until the mixture comes together into a ball.
3. Beat in the eggs one at a time, until the mixture is smooth and glossy.
4. Spoon the mixture into a piping bag and pipe 6-8 long strips onto a baking tray lined with baking paper.
5. Place the baking tray in the Ninja Dual Zone and bake for 20 minutes, or until the pastry is golden brown and puffed up. Remove from the oven and allow to cool.
6. To make the filling, whisk together the cream, sugar, and vanilla extract until stiff peaks form. Fold in the chopped chocolate.
7. Slice the cooled eclairs in half and spoon the filling into the bottom half.
8. To make the icing, mix the icing sugar, cocoa powder, and hot water until smooth. Spoon over the top of the eclairs and allow to set before serving.

Chocolate Fudge Cake

Serves: 12
Prep Time: 15 minutes
Cook Time: 35 minutes
Ninja Dual Zone mode: Bake

Ingredients:
- 214g of all-purpose flour
- 256g of granulated sugar
- 96g unsweetened cocoa powder
- 2 teaspoons baking soda
- 1 teaspoon baking powder
- 1 teaspoon salt
- 128g buttermilk, at room temperature
- 250 ml vegetable oil
- 2 large eggs, at room temperature
- 2 teaspoons vanilla extract
- 250 ml of hot water

Instructions:
1. Preheat the Ninja Dual Zone to 177°C in bake mode.
2. Grease a 9-inch round cake pan with cooking spray or butter.
3. In a large mixing bowl, whisk together flour, sugar, cocoa powder, baking soda, baking powder, and salt.
4. In a separate mixing bowl, whisk together buttermilk, vegetable oil, eggs, and vanilla extract until well combined.
5. Add the wet Ingredients to the dry Ingredients and mix until just combined.
6. Slowly pour in the hot water and stir until the batter is smooth.
7. Pour the batter into the prepared cake pan.
8. Place the cake pan in the Ninja Dual Zone and bake for 35-40 minutes or until a toothpick inserted into the centre of the cake comes out clean.
9. Remove the cake from the Ninja Dual Zone and let it cool completely on a wire rack.
10. Serve with clotted cream.

Clotted Cream

Serves: 8
Prep Time: 5 minutes
Cook Time: 8 hours
Ninja Dual Zone mode: Roast and Bake
Ingredients:
- 256g of heavy cream
- 32g sour cream

Instructions:

1. Preheat the Ninja Dual Zone to 82°C in roast mode.
2. Pour the heavy cream into a baking dish that fits inside the Ninja Dual Zone Ninja Dual .
3. Stir in the sour cream.
4. Cover the dish with foil and place it in the Ninja Dual Zone Ninja Dual .
5. Let the cream cook for 8-10 hours, until a thick layer has formed on top.
6. Remove the dish from the Ninja Dual Zone and let it cool.
7. Cover the dish with plastic wrap and refrigerate for at least 8 hours or overnight.
8. Scoop the thickened cream from the top of the dish and serve with the chocolate fudge cake.

Eccles Cake

Serves: 6
Prep Time: 20 minutes
Cook Time: 15 minutes
Ninja Dual Zone mode: Bake

Ingredients:

- 1 sheet puff pastry, thawed
- 32g unsalted butter, softened
- 32g granulated sugar
- 1/2 teaspoon ground cinnamon
- 1/4 teaspoon ground nutmeg
- 1/4 teaspoon ground allspice
- 64g currants
- 1 egg, beaten

Instructions:

1. Preheat the Ninja Dual Zone air fryer to 190°C (190°C)
2. In a mixing bowl, combine the softened butter, sugar, cinnamon, nutmeg, and allspice. Mix until well combined.
3. Stir in the currants.
4. On a floured surface, roll out the puff pastry to a thickness of about 1/8 inch.
5. Cut out 6 circles using a 4-inch cookie cutter or bowl.
6. Place a spoonful of the currant mixture onto the centre of each pastry circle.
7. Fold the pastry over the currant mixture and pinch the edges to seal.
8. Flip the pastry over and gently flatten it with the palm of your hand.
9. Use a sharp knife to make a few small slits on the top of each pastry.
10. Brush the beaten egg over the top of each pastry.
11. Place the pastries in the air fryer basket with the Ninja Dual set to "Bake" and cook for 15 minutes, or until the pastries are golden brown and crispy.
12. Remove the pastries from the air fryer and let them cool for a few minutes before serving.

Lemon Meringue Pie

Serves: 8
Prep Time: 20 minutes
Cook Time: 20-25 minutes
Ninja Dual Zone mode: Bake

Ingredients:

For the crust:

- 104g of all-purpose flour
- 64g unsalted butter, cold and cubed
- 32g granulated sugar
- 1 large egg yolk
- 1 tablespoon cold water

For the lemon filling:

- 128g granulated sugar
- 64g cornstarch
- 1/2 teaspoon salt
- 256g of water
- 6 egg yolks
- 64g fresh lemon juice
- 2 tablespoons unsalted butter

For the meringue topping:

- 6 egg whites
- 1/2 teaspoon cream of tartar
- 60g granulated sugar

Instructions:

1. Preheat the Ninja Dual Zone to 190°C in Ninja Dual mode.
2. To make the crust, combine the flour, butter, and sugar in a food processor and pulse until the mixture resembles coarse sand. Add the egg yolk and water, and pulse until the dough comes together.
3. Roll the dough out on a floured surface and transfer it to a 9-inch pie dish. Trim the edges and crimp with a fork.
4. Blind bake the crust for 10 minutes in the preheated Ninja Dual Zone . Remove the pie weights and parchment paper, and continue to bake for another 5-10 minutes, until lightly golden. Set aside to cool.
5. To make the lemon filling, whisk together the sugar,

cornstarch, and salt in a medium saucepan. Gradually whisk in the water and egg yolks until smooth.

6. Cook the mixture over medium heat, whisking constantly, until it thickens and comes to a boil. Remove from heat and stir in the lemon juice and butter.

7. Pour the lemon filling into the cooled pie crust.

8. To make the meringue topping, beat the egg whites and cream of tartar with an electric mixer until soft peaks form. Gradually add the sugar and continue to beat until stiff peaks form.

9. Spread the meringue over the lemon filling, making sure to seal the edges.

10. Bake the pie in the preheated Ninja Dual Zone for 10-12 minutes, until the meringue is lightly browned.

11. Remove from the Ninja Dual Zone and let cool completely before serving.

Pavlova

Serves: 8
Prep Time: 20 minutes
Cook Time: 1 hour 30 minutes
Ninja Dual Zone mode: Air Fry

Ingredients:
- 4 egg whites
- 128g superfine sugar
- 1 tsp white vinegar
- 1 tsp cornstarch
- 1 tsp vanilla extract
- 128g heavy cream
- Assorted fresh fruit for topping (such as strawberries, kiwi, and passionfruit)

Instructions:
1. Preheat your Ninja Dual Zone to 148°C on Air Fry mode.

2. In a large mixing bowl, whisk the egg whites until they form stiff peaks.

3. Gradually add the sugar, one tablespoon at a time, while continuing to whisk until the mixture is glossy and smooth.

4. Add the vinegar, cornstarch, and vanilla extract, and gently fold in until fully combined.

5. Spoon the mixture onto a baking tray lined with parchment paper, creating a large circular shape with a slight indentation in the centre.

6. Place the baking tray into the Ninja Dual Zone and cook in Airfryer mode at 148°C for 1 hour 30 minutes.

7. Once cooked, turn off the Ninja Dual Zone and allow the pavlova to cool completely in the oven.

8. Whip the heavy cream until it forms soft peaks.

9. Top the cooled pavlova with the whipped cream and fresh fruit.

Rhubarb Crumble

Serves: 6
Prep Time: 20 minutes
Cook Time: 40 minutes
Ninja Dual Zone mode: Bake

Ingredients:
- 500g of chopped rhubarb
- 64g granulated sugar
- 1/2 tsp ground cinnamon
- 64g all-purpose flour
- 64g rolled oats
- 64g brown sugar
- 64g unsalted butter, chilled and diced
- Whipped cream or vanilla ice cream (optional)

Instructions:
1. Preheat your Ninja Dual Zone to 190°C on Bake mode.

2. In a large mixing bowl, combine the chopped rhubarb, granulated sugar, and ground cinnamon.

3. In a separate mixing bowl, combine the flour, rolled oats, and brown sugar. Add in the chilled, diced butter and use your fingers to mix until the mixture resembles coarse breadcrumbs.

4. Spread the rhubarb mixture evenly into a 9-inch pie dish or baking dish.

5. Sprinkle the crumble mixture evenly over the top of the rhubarb.

6. Place the pie dish or baking dish into the Ninja Dual Zone and cook on Bake mode at 190°C for 40 minutes, or until the crumble is golden brown and the rhubarb is tender.

7. Serve the rhubarb crumble warm with whipped cream or vanilla ice cream if desired.

British Flapjacks

Serves: 8-10
Prep Time: 10 minutes
Cook Time: 15-20 minutes
Ninja Dual Zone mode: Bake

Ingredients:
- 174g of rolled oats
- 64g unsalted butter

- 64g light brown sugar
- 32g golden syrup
- 1/2 teaspoon salt

Instructions:

1. Preheat the Ninja Dual Zone air fryer to 177°C
2. In a mixing bowl, combine the rolled oats and salt.
3. In a saucepan, melt the butter, brown sugar, and golden syrup over medium heat, stirring until smooth.
4. Pour the melted mixture over the oats and stir until well combined.
5. Transfer the mixture to a greased 8-inch square baking dish and spread it out evenly.
6. Place the baking dish in the air fryer basket with the Ninja Dual set to "Bake" for 15-20 minutes, or until the edges are golden brown.
7. Remove the baking dish from the air fryer and let the flapjacks cool in the dish for 10-15 minutes.
8. Use a sharp knife to cut the flapjacks into squares or rectangles.
9. Let the flapjacks cool completely in the dish before serving.

Trifle

Serves: 8-10
Prep Time: 20 minutes
Cook Time: 0 minutes
Ninja Dual Zone mode: Bake or Air Fry, depending on whether the sponge cake is homemade or store-bought

Ingredients:

- 1 store-bought sponge cake or Madeira cake
- 1 can of fruit cocktail, drained
- 1 pint of fresh strawberries, sliced
- 1 pint of heavy whipping cream
- 1 package of instant vanilla pudding mix
- 128g of milk
- 32g of sugar
- 1 tsp of vanilla extract
- Shaved chocolate, for garnish

Instructions:

1. Cut the sponge cake into small cubes and arrange them at the bottom of a glass trifle bowl.
2. Add a layer of fruit cocktail over the sponge cake, followed by a layer of sliced strawberries.
3. In a separate bowl, whisk together the heavy whipping cream, sugar, and vanilla extract until stiff peaks form.
4. In another bowl, prepare the instant vanilla

pudding mix according to the package Instructions using 128g of milk.

5. Add half of the whipped cream to the pudding and fold gently until combined.
6. Spoon the pudding mixture over the strawberries in the trifle bowl.
7. Add another layer of fruit cocktail and sliced strawberries.
8. Top with the remaining whipped cream and garnish with shaved chocolate.
9. Cover and refrigerate for at least 2 hours before serving.

Victoria Sponge Cake

Serves: 8-10
Prep Time: 15 minutes
Cook Time: 20-25 minutes
Mode: Bake

Ingredients:

- 128g of unsalted butter, softened
- 128g of granulated sugar
- 4 large eggs
- 256g of self-raising flour
- 2 tsp of baking powder
- 32g of whole milk
- 64g of strawberry jam
- Powdered sugar, for dusting

Instructions:

1. Preheat the Ninja Dual Zone to 177°C on Bake mode.
2. Grease and line two 8-inch round cake pans with parchment paper.
3. In a large mixing bowl, cream the butter and sugar until light and fluffy.
4. Add the eggs one at a time, mixing well after each addition.
5. Sift in the flour and baking powder, and fold gently until combined.
6. Add the milk and mix until the batter is smooth and well combined.
7. Divide the batter evenly between the two prepared cake pans.
8. Bake for 20-25 minutes, or until a toothpick inserted in the center comes out clean.
9. Remove from the oven and let cool for 5 minutes before transferring to a wire rack to cool completely.
10. Once cooled, spread strawberry jam on one of the cakes and top with the other cake.
11. Dust with powdered sugar before serving.

Victoria Sandwich Cake

Serves: 8-10
Prep Time: 20 minutes
Cook Time: 25-30 minutes
Ninja Dual Zone mode: Bake
Ingredients:

- 128g unsalted butter, at room temperature
- 128g granulated sugar
- 4 large eggs, at room temperature
- 1 teaspoon vanilla extract
- 256g of all-purpose flour
- 2 teaspoons baking powder
- 1/2 teaspoon salt
- 64g strawberry jam
- Powdered sugar, for dusting

Instructions:

1. Preheat the Ninja Dual Zone air fryer to 165°C using the Ninja Dual feature.
2. Grease two 8-inch cake pans and line the bottom with parchment paper.
3. In a large bowl, cream together the butter and sugar until light and fluffy, using a hand mixer or stand mixer.
4. Beat in the eggs, one at a time, until fully incorporated.
5. Stir in the vanilla extract.
6. In a separate bowl, whisk together the flour, baking powder, and salt.
7. Gradually add the dry Ingredients to the wet Ingredients, mixing until just combined.
8. Divide the batter evenly between the prepared cake pans.
9. Place the cake pans in the air fryer basket with the Ninja Dual set to "Bake" for 25-30 minutes or until a toothpick inserted in the centre comes out clean.
10. Remove the cake pans from the air fryer and let the cakes cool in the pans for 10 minutes.
11. Run a knife around the edge of each cake and invert onto a wire rack to cool completely.
12. Once the cakes are cool, spread the strawberry jam on one cake and place the other cake on top.
13. Dust the top of the cake with powdered sugar before serving.

Black Forest Gateau

Serves: 8
Prep Time: 30 minutes
Cook Time: 35 minutes
Ninja Dual Zone mode: Bake
Ingredients:

- 6 large eggs, separated
- 200g caster sugar
- 175g plain flour
- 50g cocoa powder
- 2 tsp baking powder
- 400g cherries, pitted
- 3 tbsp cherry brandy (optional)
- 600ml double cream
- 1 tsp vanilla extract
- 100g dark chocolate, grated

Instructions:

1. Preheat your Ninja Dual Zone to Bake mode at 177°C.
2. Grease two 20cm round cake tins and line the bases with baking paper.
3. In a large bowl, whisk together the egg yolks and sugar until thick and creamy.
4. In a separate bowl, sift together the flour, cocoa powder and baking powder.
5. Gradually fold the flour mixture into the egg yolk mixture, taking care not to overmix.
6. In a separate bowl, whisk the egg whites until stiff peaks form.
7. Gently fold the egg whites into the cake batter.
8. Divide the mixture evenly between the two prepared cake tins and bake for 30-35 minutes or until a skewer inserted into the centre of the cakes comes out clean.
9. Remove the cakes from the oven and allow them to cool in the tins for 10 minutes before turning them out onto a wire rack to cool completely.
10. In a small bowl, mix the pitted cherries and cherry brandy, if using.
11. In a large bowl, whisk the double cream and vanilla extract until soft peaks form.
12. To assemble the gateau, place one of the cakes on a serving plate and spread a layer of whipped cream on top.

Chelsea Buns

Serves: 6-8
Prep Time: 20 minutes
Cook Time: 20 minutes
Ninja Dual Zone mode: Air Fry
Ingredients:

- 500g bread flour

- 1 tsp salt
- 75g caster sugar
- 7g sachet of fast-action yeast
- 300 ml milk, warm
- 50g unsalted butter, melted
- 1 large egg, beaten
- 200g mixed dried fruit
- 1 tsp ground cinnamon
- 25g unsalted butter, melted
- 75g demerara sugar
- Icing sugar, to dust

Instructions:

1. In a large bowl, mix the bread flour, salt, caster sugar and yeast.
2. Add the warm milk, melted butter and beaten egg to the bowl and mix until a dough forms.
3. Knead the dough on a floured surface for 10-15 minutes until smooth and elastic.
4. Place the dough in a greased bowl, cover with a tea towel and leave to rise in a warm place for 1 hour.
5. Preheat the Ninja Dual Zone to Air Fry mode at 177°C.
6. Roll out the dough into a large rectangle and sprinkle with the mixed dried fruit and ground cinnamon.
7. Roll up the dough tightly from the longest side to create a sausage shape.
8. Cut the dough into 6-8 equal slices.
9. Brush each slice with melted butter and sprinkle with demerara sugar.
10. Place the slices into the Air Fry basket and cook for 18-20 minutes until golden and cooked through.
11. Dust with icing sugar before serving.

Strawberry Fool

Serves: 4
Prep Time: 15 minutes
Cook Time: 5 minutes
Ninja Dual Zone mode: Bake
Ingredients:
- 500g fresh strawberries, hulled and quartered
- 64g granulated sugar
- 128g heavy whipping cream
- 1/2 teaspoon vanilla extract

Instructions:

1. Preheat the Ninja Dual Zone air fryer to 177°C
2. In a mixing bowl, combine the strawberries and sugar. Toss gently to coat the strawberries with the sugar.

3. Transfer the strawberry mixture to an oven-safe dish and place it in the air fryer basket.
4. Set the Ninja Dual to "Bake" and cook for 5 minutes, or until the strawberries are soft and the juices have been released.
5. Remove the dish from the air fryer and let it cool for 5 minutes.
6. In a separate mixing bowl, whip the heavy whipping cream and vanilla extract until stiff peaks form.
7. Gently fold the strawberry mixture into the whipped cream, being careful not to overmix.
8. Divide the strawberry fool mixture evenly among 4 serving dishes or glasses.
9. Refrigerate the strawberry fool for at least 1 hour before serving.

Millionaire's Shortbread

Serves: 9-12
Prep Time: 30 minutes
Cook Time: 25-30 minutes
Ninja Dual Zone mode: Bake

Ingredients:

For the shortbread:
- 104g of all-purpose flour
- 32g granulated sugar
- 1/4 teaspoon salt
- 64g unsalted butter, cold and cubed

For the caramel:
- 64g unsalted butter
- 64g light brown sugar
- 1 can of sweetened condensed milk

For the chocolate topping:
- 170 semi-sweet chocolate chips
- 1 tablespoon vegetable oil

Instructions:

1. Preheat the Ninja Dual Zone to 177°C
2. In a medium bowl, whisk together the flour, sugar, and salt for the shortbread.
3. Add the cold, cubed butter and use your hands or a pastry cutter to work the butter into the dry Ingredients until the mixture resembles coarse sand.
4. Press the mixture evenly into the bottom of an 8x8-inch baking dish. Bake for 20-25 minutes or until golden brown. Let cool for 10 minutes.
5. To make the caramel, melt the butter in a saucepan over medium heat. Add the brown sugar and condensed milk and stir constantly for 5-10 minutes until thick and bubbly.

6. Pour the caramel over the cooled shortbread and spread it out evenly. Let it cool and set for about 30 minutes.

7. To make the chocolate topping, combine the chocolate chips and vegetable oil in a microwave-safe bowl. Microwave for 30 seconds, stir, and continue microwaving and stirring in 15-second intervals until the chocolate is melted and smooth.

8. Pour the melted chocolate over the cooled caramel layer, spreading it out evenly.

9. Let the chocolate set at room temperature for at least 1 hour, or in the refrigerator for 20-30 minutes.

10. Cut the millionaire's shortbread into squares and serve.

Peach Melba

Serves: 4-6
Prep Time: 15 minutes
Cook Time: 10-12 minutes
Ninja Dual Zone mode: Air Fry

Ingredients:
- 4 ripe peaches, halved and pitted
- 34 granulated sugar
- 1 teaspoon vanilla extract
- 64g raspberry jam
- 1 tablespoon water
- Vanilla ice cream, to serve
- Fresh raspberries, to serve
- Mint leaves, to garnish

Instructions:
1. Preheat the Ninja Dual Zone to 190°C on Air Fry mode.

2. In a small bowl, whisk together the sugar and vanilla extract.

3. Dip the peach halves in the sugar mixture, making sure they are coated on both sides.

4. Place the peaches, cut side down, in the air fryer basket. Air fry for 10-12 minutes, or until the peaches are soft and caramelized.

5. Meanwhile, in a small saucepan, heat the raspberry jam and water over medium heat until the jam is melted and smooth.

6. To serve, place a peach half in each bowl or on a plate. Drizzle with the raspberry sauce and top with a scoop of vanilla ice cream, fresh raspberries, and a mint leaf.

7. Serve immediately.

Custard Tart

Serves: 8
Prep Time: 15 minutes
Cook Time: 30 minutes
Ninja Dual Zone mode: Bake

Ingredients:
- 1 sheet of frozen shortcrust pastry, thawed
- 256g of milk
- 4 egg yolks
- 64g of sugar
- 1 teaspoon of vanilla extract
- Ground nutmeg
- Fresh berries for serving

Instructions:
1. Preheat the Ninja Dual Zone to Bake mode at 177°C.

2. Grease a 9-inch tart pan and line it with the shortcrust pastry. Trim any excess pastry hanging over the edge.

3. In a mixing bowl, whisk the egg yolks, sugar, and vanilla extract until they're combined.

4. In a saucepan, heat the milk until it starts to steam, then pour it into the mixing bowl with the egg yolk mixture while whisking.

5. Once combined, pour the custard mixture into the prepared tart pan.

6. Sprinkle the top of the custard with ground nutmeg.

7. Bake the custard tart for 30 minutes or until the custard is set and the pastry is golden brown.

8. Once cooked, remove the custard tart from the Ninja Dual Zone and let it cool completely.

9. Serve with fresh berries.

Summer Pudding

Serves: 6
Prep Time: 20 minutes
Cook Time: 10 minutes
Chill time: 3 hours
Ninja Dual Zone mode: Bake

Ingredients:
- 400g mixed fresh berries (strawberries, raspberries, blackberries, and blueberries)
- 64g of sugar
- 4-5 slices of white bread, crusts removed
- Extra berries for serving

Instructions:
1. Preheat the Ninja Dual Zone to Bake mode at

177°C.

2. In a saucepan, combine the mixed berries and sugar and cook over medium heat until the sugar dissolves and the berries release their juices.

3. Cut the bread into thin slices and use them to line a 6-cup pudding basin, ensuring there are no gaps between the slices.

4. Pour the warm berry mixture into the bread-lined basin, reserving a little juice to pour over the top.

5. Cover the top of the basin with more slices of bread, again ensuring there are no gaps.

6. Cover the basin with cling film and place a small plate on top to weigh it down.

7. Place the basin in the Ninja Dual Zone and bake for 10 minutes or until the bread is slightly toasted.

8. Remove the basin from the Ninja Dual Zone and let it cool, then refrigerate for at least 3 hours.

9. To serve, turn the pudding out onto a plate and top it with extra berries and reserved juice.

Treacle Tart

Serves: 6-8
Prep Time: 15 minutes
Cook Time: 25 minutes
Ninja Dual Zone mode: Air Fry

Ingredients:

- 375g shortcrust pastry
- 200g golden syrup
- 100g breadcrumbs
- Zest of 1 lemon
- 1 egg, beaten

Instructions:

1. Preheat the Ninja Dual Zone air fryer to 177°C.

2. Roll out the shortcrust pastry on a lightly floured surface and use it to line a 23cm tart tin.

3. In a mixing bowl, combine the golden syrup, breadcrumbs, and lemon zest.

4. Pour the mixture into the tart tin and spread it out evenly.

5. Brush the edges of the pastry with beaten egg.

6. Roll out the remaining pastry and use it to make a lattice on top of the tart, trimming off any excess pastry.

7. Brush the lattice with a beaten egg.

8. Place the tart in the Ninja Dual Zone air fryer and cook for 25 minutes or until golden brown and crisp.

9. Remove the tart from the air fryer and allow it to cool before serving.

Apple Pie

Serves: 8
Prep Time: 30 minutes
Cook Time: 45 minutes
Ninja Dual Zone mode: Air Fry

Ingredients:

- 500g shortcrust pastry
- 6 medium-sized apples, peeled and cored
- 75g caster sugar
- 1 tsp ground cinnamon
- 1/4 tsp ground nutmeg
- 2 tbsp plain flour
- 1 egg, beaten
- 1 tbsp demerara sugar

Instructions:

1. Preheat the Ninja Dual Zone air fryer to 177°C.

2. Roll out half of the shortcrust pastry on a lightly floured surface and use it to line a 23cm pie dish.

3. In a mixing bowl, toss together the apples, caster sugar, cinnamon, nutmeg, and flour.

4. Pour the apple mixture into the pastry-lined pie dish.

5. Roll out the remaining pastry and use it to make a lattice on top of the pie, trimming off any excess pastry.

6. Brush the lattice with beaten egg and sprinkle with demerara sugar.

7. Place the pie in the Ninja Dual Zone air fryer and cook for 45 minutes or until golden brown and the apples are tender.

8. Remove the pie from the air fryer and allow it to cool before serving.

Chocolate Brownies

Serves: 9
Prep Time: 10 minutes
Cook Time: 25-30 minutes
Ninja Dual Zone mode: Bake

Ingredients:

- 64g unsalted butter, melted
- 128g granulated sugar
- 2 large eggs
- 1 tsp vanilla extract
- 64g all-purpose flour
- 45g unsweetened cocoa powder
- 1/4 tsp salt
- 1/4 tsp baking powder

- 64g semi-sweet chocolate chips

Instructions:

1. Preheat the Ninja Dual Zone to 177°C
2. Grease an 8-inch square baking pan with cooking spray.
3. In a large bowl, mix melted butter and sugar until combined.
4. Beat in eggs and vanilla extract.
5. In a separate bowl, whisk together flour, cocoa powder, salt, and baking powder.
6. Gradually mix the dry Ingredients into the wet Ingredients until just combined.
7. Fold in chocolate chips.
8. Pour the batter into the prepared baking pan and smooth the top with a spatula.
9. Bake for 25-30 minutes or until a toothpick inserted in the centre comes out clean.
10. Remove from the oven and let it cool completely in the pan.
11. Cut into 9 squares and serve.

Christmas Pudding

Serves: 8-10
Prep Time: 20 minutes
Cook Time: 1 hour 30 minutes
Ninja Dual Zone mode:Bake
Ingredients:

- 128g raisins
- 128g currants
- 128g chopped mixed peel
- 64g chopped almonds
- 64g dark brown sugar
- 64g all-purpose flour
- 1/2 tsp ground cinnamon
- 1/2 tsp ground nutmeg
- 1/2 tsp ground cloves
- 1/2 tsp baking soda
- 1/2 tsp salt
- 2 eggs, beaten
- 125 ml milk
- 32g unsalted butter, melted
- 60 ml brandy
- Zest of 1 orange

Instructions:

1. Preheat the Ninja Dual Zone to 165°C
2. Grease a 2-quart pudding basin with butter or cooking spray.
3. In a large bowl, mix raisins, currants, mixed peel,

chopped almonds, and dark brown sugar.
4. In another bowl, whisk together flour, cinnamon, nutmeg, cloves, baking soda, and salt.
5. Mix the dry Ingredients into the fruit mixture until well combined.
6. In a separate bowl, whisk together eggs, milk, melted butter, brandy, and orange zest.
7. Gradually mix the wet Ingredients into the fruit mixture until everything is well combined.
8. Pour the mixture into the prepared pudding basin and cover it with a lid or a piece of foil.
9. Place the pudding basin on the trivet in the Ninja Dual Zone Ninja Dual .
10. Fill the Ninja Dual Zone with hot water until it reaches halfway up the sides of the pudding basin.
11. Cover the Ninja Dual Zone with the lid and bake for 1 hour and 30 minutes.
12. Once done, remove the pudding basin from the Ninja Dual Zone and allow it to cool for 10 minutes.
13. Turn the pudding onto a plate and serve with custard or whipped cream.

Rustic Stuffed Pears

Serves: 4
Prep Time: 5 minutes
Cook Time: 18 minutes
Ninja Dual Zone mode: Bake

Ingredients

- 4 medium baking pears
- 80g quick-cooking oats
- 60g almonds, chopped
- 50g raisins
- 20g honey
- 1 tbsp candied orange peel
- 1 tsp cinnamon powder

Instructions:

1. Remove the stems and seeds from the pears; scoop out the flesh using a spoon.
2. In a mixing bowl, thoroughly combine the remaining Ingredients. Spoon the filling mixture into the prepared pears.
3. Place the pears in both drawers.
4. Select zone 1 and pair it with "BAKE" at 170°C for 18 minutes. Select "MATCH" followed by the "START/STOP" button.
5. Serve stuffed pears warm or at room temperature. Enjoy!

Chapter 7: Sauces, Dips and Dressings

Sweet Potatoes

Prep Time: 10 minutes
Cook Time: 20-25 minutes
Serves: 4
Ninja Dual Zone mode: Air Fry

Ingredients:
- 4 medium-sized sweet potatoes
- 2 tablespoons olive oil
- 1 teaspoon salt
- 1/2 teaspoon black pepper
- Optional: additional herbs or seasonings of your choice (such as rosemary, thyme, garlic powder, or paprika)

Preparation Instructions:
1. Preheat your Ninja Dual Zone in the air fry mode according to the manufacturer's instructions.
2. Wash and scrub the potatoes to remove any dirt. You can peel them if desired, but leaving the skin on adds extra texture and flavour.
3. Cut the potatoes into wedges or cubes, keeping them a similar size for even cooking.
4. Place the potato wedges or cubes in a bowl and drizzle them with olive oil. Toss them gently to coat the potatoes evenly.
5. Season the potatoes with salt, black pepper, and any additional herbs or seasonings you prefer. Mix well to ensure the seasoning is evenly distributed.
6. Open the Ninja Dual Zone and carefully place the seasoned potatoes in the air frying zone.
7. Set the temperature to around 200°C and the cooking time to approximately 20-25 minutes, or until the potatoes are golden brown and crispy. Cooking times may vary depending on the size of the potato pieces and the desired level of crispiness, so monitor them closely.
8. Once the potatoes are cooked to your liking, remove them from the Ninja Dual Zone using oven mitts or tongs.
9. Allow the roasted potatoes to cool slightly before serving. They make a delicious side dish or snack.

Caesar Dressing

Prep Time: 10 minutes
Cook Time: No cooking required
Servings: 4
Ninja Dual Zone mode: None

Ingredients:
- 120ml mayonnaise
- 2 tablespoons freshly squeezed lemon juice
- 2 teaspoons Dijon mustard
- 2 cloves garlic, minced
- 2 anchovy fillets, finely chopped (optional)
- 28g grated Parmesan cheese
- 1/4 teaspoon salt
- 1/4 teaspoon black pepper
- 60ml extra-virgin olive oil

Preparation Instructions:
1. Place the mayonnaise, lemon juice, Dijon mustard, minced garlic, anchovy fillets (if using), Parmesan cheese, salt, and black pepper into your blender
2. Secure the lid on the blender and turn it on.
3. Start blending on a low speed and gradually increase the speed until all the Ingredients are well combined and smooth.
4. While the blender is running, slowly drizzle in the extra-virgin olive oil until the dressing emulsifies and thickens.
5. Stop the blender and scrape down the sides of the pitcher with a spatula, if necessary.
6. Taste the dressing and adjust the seasoning if needed, adding more lemon juice, salt, or black pepper to your preference.
7. Pour the Caesar dressing into a jar or airtight container and refrigerate for at least 30 minutes to allow the flavours to meld together.
8. Serve the Caesar dressing over crisp romaine lettuce, croutons, and additional grated Parmesan cheese if desired.

Crispy chicken strips with dipping sauce

Serves: 4
Prep Time: 15 minutes
Cook Time: 8-10 minutes
Ninja Dual Zone mode: Air Fry

Ingredients:
- 500g chicken breast, cut into strips
- 128g flour
- 1 tsp garlic powder
- 1 tsp onion powder
- 1 tsp paprika
- 1 tsp salt
- 1/2 tsp black pepper
- 2 eggs, beaten
- 256g of panko bread crumbs
- Cooking spray
- Dipping sauce of your choice

Instructions:
1. Preheat the Ninja Dual Zone to 190°C using the Air Fry mode.
2. In a shallow dish, mix the flour, garlic powder, onion powder, paprika, salt, and black pepper.
3. In another shallow dish, beat the eggs.
4. In a third shallow dish, place the panko breadcrumbs.
5. Dip each chicken strip into the flour mixture, then into the beaten eggs, and then coat well with the panko breadcrumbs.
6. Place the coated chicken strips onto the air fryer basket in a single layer, making sure they don't touch.
7. Spray the chicken strips with cooking spray.
8. Air fry for 8-10 minutes or until golden brown and cooked through, flipping halfway through cooking.
9. Serve with your favourite dipping sauce.

Chocolate Chip Cookies

Prep Time: 15 minutes
Cook Time: 8-10 minutes
Serves: around 24 cookies
Ninja Dual Zone mode: Baking

Ingredients:
- 226g unsalted butter, softened
- 200g granulated sugar
- 220g packed brown sugar
- 2 large eggs
- 1 teaspoon vanilla extract
- 375g all-purpose flour
- 1 teaspoon baking soda
- 1/2 teaspoon salt
- 340g chocolate chips

Preparation Instructions:
1. Preheat your Ninja Dual Zone in the baking mode according to the manufacturer's instructions.
2. In a large mixing bowl, cream together the softened butter, granulated sugar, and brown sugar until light and fluffy.
3. Add the eggs one at a time, beating well after each addition. Stir in the vanilla extract.
4. In a separate bowl, whisk together the flour, baking soda, and salt.
5. Gradually add the dry Ingredients to the wet Ingredients, mixing until just combined. Do not overmix. Fold in the chocolate chips.
6. Drop rounded tablespoons or use a cookie scoop to portion the dough onto a baking sheet, leaving some space between each cookie.
7. Open the Ninja Dual Zone and carefully place the baking sheet with the cookie dough on the appropriate baking zone.
8. Set the temperature to around 175°C and the cooking time to approximately 8-10 minutes, or until the edges of the cookies are golden brown. The centres may appear slightly undercooked but will firm up as they cool.
9. Once the cookies are baked to your liking, remove the baking sheet from the Ninja Dual Zone using oven mitts or a heat-safe spatula.
10. Allow the cookies to cool on the baking sheet for a few minutes, then transfer them to a wire rack to cool completely.

Zucchini Fritters

Prep Time: 15 minutes
Cook Time: 10-12 minutes
Serves: around 12 fritters
Ninja Dual Zone mode: Air Fry

Ingredients:
- 2 medium zucchini
- 1 teaspoon salt
- 60g all-purpose flour
- 25g grated Parmesan cheese

- 2 cloves garlic, minced
- 1/4 teaspoon black pepper
- 2 large eggs, beaten
- Olive oil, for brushing

Preparation Instructions:

1. Preheat your Ninja Dual Zone in the air fry mode according to the manufacturer's instructions.
2. Grate the zucchini using a box grater or a food processor. Place the grated zucchini in a colander and sprinkle with salt. Let it sit for about 10 minutes to allow the excess moisture to drain.
3. After 10 minutes, squeeze out the excess moisture from the grated zucchini using a clean kitchen towel or your hands.
4. In a large mixing bowl, combine the grated zucchini, flour, grated Parmesan cheese, minced garlic, black pepper, and beaten eggs. Mix until well combined.
5. Take a portion of the zucchini mixture and shape it into a patty using your hands. Place the formed fritters on a plate.
6. Open the Ninja Dual Zone and carefully place the zucchini fritters in the air frying zone. Depending on the size of your Ninja Dual Zone, you may need to cook them in batches.
7. Lightly brush the tops of the fritters with olive oil to help promote browning.
8. Set the temperature to around 190°C and the cooking time to approximately 10-12 minutes, or until the fritters are golden brown and crispy. Flip them halfway through the cooking time for even browning.
9. Once the fritters are cooked to your liking, remove them from the Ninja Dual Zone using oven mitts or a heat-safe spatula.
10. Allow the zucchini fritters to cool slightly before serving. They are delicious as a side dish or as part of a brunch spread. You can also serve them with a dipping sauce of your choice, such as tzatziki or sour cream.

Apologies for the confusion. Here's a recipe for Roasted Red Pepper Sauce using the Ninja Dual Zone:

Prep Time: 10 minutes
Cook Time: 20 minutes
Total Time: 30 minutes
Serves: 4

Ninja Dual Zone mode: Roast
Ingredients:
- 2 large red bell peppers
- 2 tablespoons olive oil
- 2 cloves garlic, minced
- 1 tablespoon balsamic vinegar
- Salt and pepper to taste

Preparation Instructions:

1. Preheat the Ninja Dual Zone to the Roast mode.
2. Cut the red bell peppers in half lengthwise and remove the stems and seeds.
3. Place the bell pepper halves on the cooking racks or in the air frying basket of the Ninja Dual Zone.
4. Drizzle the bell peppers with 1 tablespoon of olive oil and season with salt and pepper.
5. Set the cooking time to 20 minutes.
6. Start the cooking process and allow the peppers to roast until the skins are charred and blistered.
7. Once the peppers are done roasting, carefully remove them from the Ninja Dual Zone and place them in a heatproof bowl.
8. Cover the bowl with plastic wrap or place them in a sealed plastic bag to steam for about 10 minutes. This will make it easier to remove the skins.
9. After steaming, carefully peel off the charred skins from the peppers.
10. Transfer the roasted red peppers to a blender or food processor.
11. Add the minced garlic, balsamic vinegar, remaining 1 tablespoon of olive oil, salt, and pepper to taste.
12. Blend the mixture until smooth and creamy. If the sauce seems too thick, you can add a little water or olive oil to achieve the desired consistency.
13. Taste and adjust the seasonings as needed.
14. Transfer the roasted red pepper sauce to a serving bowl or storage container.
15. The sauce can be served immediately or refrigerated for later use.

BBQ Sauce

Prep Time: 5 minutes
Cook Time: 10 minutes
Total Time: 15 minutes
Serves: 4

Ninja Dual Zone mode: Air Fry

Ingredients:

- 240mls ketchup
- 2 tablespoons brown sugar
- 1 tablespoon Worcestershire sauce
- 1 tablespoon apple cider vinegar
- 1 teaspoon Dijon mustard
- 1/2 teaspoon smoked paprika
- 1/4 teaspoon garlic powder
- 1/4 teaspoon onion powder
- Salt and pepper to taste

Preparation Instructions:

1. In a small bowl, combine all the Ingredients: ketchup, brown sugar, Worcestershire sauce, apple cider vinegar, Dijon mustard, smoked paprika, garlic powder, onion powder, salt, and pepper. Stir well to combine.
2. Preheat the Ninja Dual Zone to the Air Fry mode.
3. Pour the BBQ sauce into a heatproof dish that fits in the air frying basket of the Ninja Dual Zone.
4. Place the dish with the BBQ sauce in the air frying basket.
5. Set the cooking time to 10 minutes.
6. Start the cooking process and allow the sauce to air fry until it thickens slightly and the flavours meld together.
7. After the cooking time is complete, carefully remove the dish from the Ninja Dual Zone using oven mitts or tongs, as it will be hot.
8. Let the BBQ sauce cool slightly before transferring it to a serving container.
9. The air-fried BBQ sauce is now ready to be used as a dip or marinade for your favourite dishes.

Dehydrated Fruit Chutney

Prep Time: 10 minutes
Cook Time: 4-6 hours (depending on the dehydrating mode)
Serves: Makes about 1 cup
Ninja Dual Zone mode: Dehydration

Ingredients:

- 340g mixed dried fruits (such as apricots, raisins, dates)
- 1 small onion, finely chopped
- 50g brown sugar
- 60ml apple cider vinegar
- 1/4 teaspoon ground cinnamon

- 1/4 teaspoon ground ginger
- Pinch of cayenne pepper
- Salt to taste

Preparation Instructions:

1. In a mixing bowl, combine the mixed dried fruits, finely chopped onion, brown sugar, apple cider vinegar, ground cinnamon, ground ginger, pinch of cayenne pepper, and salt. Stir well to ensure all the Ingredients are evenly distributed.
2. Preheat the Ninja Dual Zone to the Dehydrate mode.
3. Spread the mixed fruit mixture in a single layer on the dehydrating trays or racks of the Ninja Dual Zone.
4. Set the dehydrating time to 4-6 hours, depending on the desired level of dehydration and the recommended settings for your specific appliance.
5. Start the dehydrating process and allow the fruit mixture to dehydrate until it becomes dry and leathery, with no moisture remaining.
6. After the dehydrating time is complete, carefully remove the trays or racks from the Ninja Dual Zone using oven mitts or tongs, as they will be hot.
7. Let the dehydrated fruit mixture cool completely before transferring it to an airtight container.
8. The dehydrated fruit chutney is now ready to be enjoyed as a condiment or snack. It can be stored in a cool, dry place for several weeks.

Blue Cheese Dip

Prep Time: 10 minutes
Cook Time: 15 minutes
Serves: 4
Ninja Dual Zone mode: Bake

Ingredients:

- 112g blue cheese crumbles
- 120g sour cream
- 60g mayonnaise
- 60ml buttermilk
- 1 tablespoon lemon juice
- 1 clove garlic, minced
- 1/4 teaspoon black pepper
- Fresh herbs (such as chives or parsley) for garnish (optional)

Preparation Instructions:

1. Preheat the Ninja Dual Zone in the Bake mode.

2. In a mixing bowl, combine the blue cheese crumbles, sour cream, mayonnaise, buttermilk, lemon juice, minced garlic, and black pepper. Stir well to thoroughly combine the Ingredients.

3. Transfer the blue cheese mixture to an oven-safe dish or ramekin that fits in the Ninja Dual Zone.

4. Place the dish with the blue cheese dip in the baking area of the Ninja Dual Zone.

5. Set the cooking time to 15 minutes.

6. Start the cooking process and allow the dip to bake until it is hot and bubbly.

7. After the baking time is complete, carefully remove the dish from the Ninja Dual Zone using oven mitts or tongs, as it will be hot.

8. Let the blue cheese dip cool slightly before serving.

9. Garnish with fresh herbs, if desired.

10. The baked blue cheese dip is now ready to be enjoyed with your favourite dippers, such as celery sticks, carrot sticks, or crackers.

Buffalo Chicken Dip

Prep Time: 15 minutes
Cook Time: 20 minutes
Serves: 6-8
Ninja Dual Zone mode: Bake

Ingredients:

- 280g chicken, shredded or diced
- 120g hot sauce (such as Frank's RedHot)
- 120g cheese dressing
- 110g cream cheese, softened
- 120g sour cream
- 112g shredded cheddar cheese
- 28g crumbled blue cheese
- 2 green onions, sliced
- Tortilla chips, celery sticks, or crackers for serving

Preparation Instructions:

1. Preheat the Ninja Dual Zone in the Bake mode.

2. In a mixing bowl, combine the cooked chicken, hot sauce, blue cheese dressing, cream cheese, and sour cream. Stir well to thoroughly combine all the Ingredients.

3. Transfer the chicken mixture to an oven-safe dish or baking pan that fits in the Ninja Dual Zone.

4. Spread the mixture evenly in the dish and sprinkle shredded cheddar cheese and crumbled blue cheese on top.

5. Place the dish with the dip in the baking area of the Ninja Dual Zone.

6. Set the cooking time to 20 minutes.

7. Start the cooking process and allow the dip to bake until it is hot and bubbly, and the cheese is melted and slightly golden.

8. After the baking time is complete, carefully remove the dish from the Ninja Dual Zone using oven mitts or tongs, as it will be hot.

9. Let the Buffalo Chicken Dip cool slightly before serving.

10. Garnish with sliced green onions.

11. Serve with tortilla chips, celery sticks, or crackers.

Balsamic Glaze

Prep Time: 5 minutes
Cook Time: 20 minutes
Serves: About ¼ cup
Ninja Dual Zone mode: Bake

Ingredients:

- 120ml balsamic vinegar

Preparation Instructions:

1. Preheat the Ninja Dual Zone in the Bake mode.

2. Pour the balsamic vinegar into a small saucepan.

3. Place the saucepan in the baking area of the Ninja Dual Zone.

4. Set the cooking time to 20 minutes.

5. Start the cooking process and allow the balsamic vinegar to simmer and reduce until it thickens into a glaze consistency. Stir occasionally.

6. After the cooking time is complete, carefully remove the saucepan from the Ninja Dual Zone using oven mitts or tongs, as it will be hot.

7. Let the balsamic glaze cool before using.

8. The balsamic glaze is now ready to be drizzled over roasted vegetables, grilled meats, or used in various recipes.

Cock-a-Leekie Soup

Prep Time: 15 minutes
Cook Time: 1 hour 30 minutes
Servings: 6
Ninja Dual Zone mode: Broil for the chicken

Ingredients:

- 1 whole chicken, about 4 pounds
- 2 leeks, white and light green parts only, thinly

sliced
- 2 carrots, peeled and diced
- 2 celery stalks, diced
- 1 onion, diced
- 2 cloves garlic, minced
- 1890g chicken broth
- 1 bay leaf
- 1 teaspoon dried thyme
- Salt and pepper to taste
- 190g cooked barley or rice (optional)
- Chopped fresh parsley for garnish

Preparation Instructions:
1. Add the leeks, carrots, celery, onion, and garlic to the cooking pot and sauté for about 5 minutes until the vegetables soften.
2. While the vegetables are sautéing, rinse the chicken under cold water and remove any giblets. Place the whole chicken on top of the sautéed vegetables in the cooking pot.
3. Pour in the chicken broth and add the bay leaf and dried thyme. Season with salt and pepper to taste.
4. Using the Broil mode on the Ninja Dual Zone, Cook for 1 hour and 30 minutes or until the chicken is cooked through and tender.
5. Carefully remove the chicken from the cooking pot and place it on a cutting board. Allow it to cool slightly.
6. While the chicken is cooling, skim any excess fat from the surface of the soup.
7. Once the chicken is cool enough to handle, remove the skin and bones. Shred the chicken meat into bite-sized pieces and return it to the soup.
8. If desired, stir in cooked barley or rice to the soup.
9. Taste the soup and adjust the seasoning as needed.
10. Ladle the Cock-a-Leekie Soup into bowls and garnish with chopped fresh parsley.
11. Serve hot and enjoy!

Honey Mustard Glaze
Prep Time: 5 minutes
Cook Time: 15 minutes
Serves: Approximately 1/2 cup
Ninja Dual Zone mode: Bake

Ingredients:
- 84g honey
- 60g Dijon mustard
- 1 tablespoon mayonnaise
- 1 tablespoon lemon juice

Preparation Instructions:
1. Preheat the Ninja Dual Zone in the Bake mode.
2. In a small bowl, whisk together the honey, Dijon mustard, mayonnaise, and lemon juice until well combined.
3. Transfer the mixture to a saucepan.
4. Place the saucepan in the baking area of the Ninja Dual Zone.
5. Set the cooking time to 15 minutes.
6. Start the cooking process and allow the honey mustard glaze to heat through and thicken slightly.
7. After the cooking time is complete, carefully remove the saucepan from the Ninja Dual Zone using oven mitts or tongs, as it will be hot.
8. Let the honey mustard glaze cool before using.
9. The honey mustard glaze is now ready to be brushed onto roasted or baked chicken, salmon, or vegetables.

Printed in Great Britain
by Amazon